$\mathcal{E}$CHOES
of the
$\mathcal{H}$UNT

a TEXAN TOLD
TRUE TALE

STAN CORVIN, JR.

2018

SOUTHWESTERN
LEGACY PRESS

ACKNOWLEDGMENTS:
Design Services: Melinda Martin, MartinPublishingServices.com

PUBLISHING INFORMATION:
NLT - New Living Translation, copyright © 1996, 2004, 2015 by Tyndale House Foundation, Carol Stream, IL 60188
NKJV - Scripture is taken from the New King James Version ® copyright © 1982 by Thomas Nelson, all rights reserved.

ISBN: 978-0-9989222-4-9 paperback, 978-0-9989222-6-3 epub,
        978-0-9989222-7-0 hardback

PUBLISHED BY: Southwestern Legacy Press
                    8901 Tehama Ridge Parkway
                    Suite 127-115
                    Fort Worth, TX 76177
                    www.swlegacypress.com

LIBRARY CATALOGING:
Names: Corvin, Stanley E. (Stanley E. Corvin, Jr.)
Echoes of the Hunt/Stan Corvin, Jr.
150 pages 23 cm x 15 cm (9 in. x 6in.)
Description: *Echoes of the Hunt* is the story of Stan Corvin's childhood memories of hunting episodes with members of his family while growing up in West Texas. The stories are interwoven with a description of the last deer hunt he was on a few years ago near Aspermont, Texas and are his memories and recollections while alone on a mountain butte, sitting in a cold deer stand and hunting a massive mule deer buck known as "El Viejo." He also reminisces about past hunting trips while relaxing in a creaking rocker, before a crackling fireplace in the evenings drinking his favorite beverage, Dr. Pepper.
Key Words: Texas Deer Hunting, Youth Hunting, Shooting Sports, Quail Hunting, Goose Hunting, Duck Hunting.

THE MULE DEER

"EL VIEJO" SUDDENLY BURST OUT of a nearby, large stand of cedar bushes and nearly ran over me. Jumping aside, I raised my rifle and turned to fire at him. Then, I heard a "bloodcurdling" guttural, deep growl close behind me. The sound made the hairs on the back of my neck stand up. With my rifle at my shoulder, very slowly I turned around and saw the large snarling cougar ten feet away with his teeth bared. He was lying down on his haunches ready to pounce, his long tail nervously twitching from side to side and staring intently at me with his large yellow eyes. When I pointed the rifle at the big cat, I realized the scope was set on twelve power, and I could not see the crosshairs to take the shot because he was too close. Sliding the safety off with my right thumb, it made a soft "click." Instantly, the big cat lunged forward and brushed past my right leg in pursuit of the deer. Swinging around, I fired at the rear of the fleeing cougar and saw the bullet strike the ground to its right. "Well, crap." I thought, as I quickly worked the bolt, ejecting and loading another shell. Then everything was quiet, and both animals were gone. Standing there, I didn't know what to do next as my heart pounded rapidly in my chest.

After a while, I walked back to the pop-up stand. Sitting down, I knew there was no point in staying at the blind because "El Viejo" and the big cougar were long gone. Finally catching my breath, I gathered up everything, put my backpack on and walked to the truck. Starting it, I thought, "Nobody will ever believe me when I tell them about this." What had just happened was a once in a lifetime set of circumstances that few hunters ever get to experience and I began to smile thinking about it.

A TEXAN'S ELEGY

Under the West Texas, pale blue sky,
Do place my grave when I die.
Joyously I lived, and joyously I died,
And my duty I did fulfill.

This be the verse you write for me,
Here he lies where he loved to be.
Home is the pilot from across the sea,
And the hunter home from the hill.

— Robert Louis Stevenson's "Requiem" Paraphrased

To my beloved wife Peggy,
who is the light of my life
and a fierce Spiritual Warrior.

I will always love you!

OTHER BOOKS BY STAN CORVIN, JR.

Vietnam Saga:
Exploits of a Combat Helicopter Pilot

Jet Pioneer: A Fighter Pilot's Memoir
By General Carl G. Schneider
With Stan Corvin, Jr.

Contents

PROLOGUE

"The Old Man used to say that the best part of hunting was the thinking about going and the talking about it after you got back. You just had to have the actual middle as a basis of conversation and to put some meat in the pot. "Everybody," he said, "should be allowed to brag some about what he did good that day, and to cover up shameless on what he did wrong."[1]

—The Old Man and the Boy
by Robert C. Ruark, Jr.

INTRODUCTION

IN AVIATION TERMS, MY LIFE is on its "final approach" as I near the end of what has been an amazing journey. It is impossible to describe the gratitude I feel for the blessed life I have lived. Oh, it has not always been easy, not by a long shot; but God's hand gently nudged me along the right path, though I frequently stumbled and Jesus always had my back even when I "made my bed in hell" as Psalm 139:8 says.

Nearing my "expiration date," as a good friend of mine calls death, I want to write about several men in my family with whom I had a close relationship and who were instrumental in developing my love of the outdoors and the sport of hunting and shooting. Although now long dead, specifically they are; my maternal grandfather Jesse H. Heath; my uncle W.J. (Jesse) Heath; my father Stan Corvin, Sr. and lastly my uncle by marriage Ewing F. ("Mac") McEntire. Collectively, and individually, they showed great patience and gave gentle instruction as they introduced me to hunting and the shooting of ducks, quail, dove, geese, deer and various "varmints." Some chapters in the book include stories about my father-in-law Roy B. Gates, also deceased. Now that I am in my seventh decade of living on this planet, I miss them more each day and look forward to the time when we can all be together again, sitting around a campfire, telling tall tales in the best hunting place of all; Heaven.

In 1944, my dad and several other United States Army Air Force (USAAF) fighter pilots arrived in Fort Worth, Texas from England to pick up new P-51D airplanes built in a plant located there.

After graduating from college a year earlier, my mother worked at the same aircraft plant and lived with two "old maid" aunts, who also worked there. On my dad's third trip back to Texas to pick up more fighter aircraft, he and my mother dated again while he was in town. They married and nine months later, I was born on May 8, 1945. At the time of my birth, my dad was on the island of Iwo Jima flying P-51D's from the airfield, after the island was secured by the marines.

My mother was the oldest of four siblings, and for three years, I was the only child in the family. As a result, I had the undivided attention of my parents, grandparents, aunts, and uncles. My dad returned from World War II, shortly after Japan surrendered on September 2, 1945. Then in 1950, he was recalled back into the US Air Force to fly F-80's, F-84's and F-86's jet aircraft during the Korean Conflict. My mother, little sister and I moved, from Austin to Colorado City, Texas, where we lived with my maternal grandparents while he was overseas.

After moving in with them, my grandfather began taking me with him as his oil company drilled wells at various ranch locations in West Texas. I frequently napped in the back seat of his car or slept in the "doghouse" which was a heated and air-conditioned, small-attached structure, built on a drilling rig platform, where crews could change clothes. I loved the outdoors and the company of "old men" as I viewed everyone with whom I was in contact, although most of the workers were probably quite young.

As I did in my earlier published book *Vietnam Saga: Exploits of a Combat Helicopter Pilot*, I am writing in essay style with each chapter containing stories about hunting episodes. The stories are interwoven with my description of the last deer hunt I was on a few years ago in West Texas and are my memories and recollections while alone on a mountain butte, sitting in a cold deer stand and hunting a massive mule deer buck known as "El Viejo."

I also reminisce about past hunts while relaxing in a creaking rocker, before a crackling fireplace in the evenings drinking my favorite beverage, Dr. Pepper.

CHAPTER ONE

FIRST DAY ARRIVAL

SITTING ON A WIND GNARLED cedar stump, at the top of "Double Mountain" Butte, I picked up my thermos, poured a cup of hot coffee and slowly sipped it as I viewed the vast open plain stretching out below through binoculars. It was late fall, the clouds were darkening and the wind, smelling of rain, had shifted to the north meaning another cold front, called a "blue northern," was coming soon. A few weeks earlier, I had been invited to hunt deer at a friend's ranch, named "Rancho Venado Grande" (Spanish: Big Deer Ranch), near Aspermont, Texas. Shortly before my arrival, he called me on my cell phone to tell me that he had the flu and would not be coming after all and that I would have the "run of the place" for the week I was there.

I arrived in early afternoon and found the cabin unlocked and stocked with food and plenty of wood for the fireplace. My friend Charlie had also told me to watch for "El Viejo," a huge mule deer buck with multiple points on his bifurcated horns and a large drop tine on each side. It had recently been spotted during the rut at an electric game feeder near the bank of the Double Mountain Fork Brazos River, which ran through the ranch. Over the past eight years, the big buck had occasionally been seen and once dimly photographed by a game camera that was slightly out of focus; but no one had gotten a shot at him. Intending to be the one who harvested the "Old Man" as the Spanish name translated into English, I chuckled to myself at the thought of one "Old Man" hunting another "Old Man." How droll! Slowly sipping the coffee, my thoughts drifted back to an earlier time, long ago, when I was five years old.

LATE FALL DUCK HUNT

I WAS SHIVERING FROM THE cold, and the anticipation of shooting my first duck while sitting in a makeshift duck blind, wrapped inside my grandfather's fleece lined overcoat. Perched on his lap, with my face peeking out, peering intently at the dark black star-filled sky and the colorful wooden decoys gently bobbing in the water a few yards away, I anxiously awaited the birds' arrival. The sun was just beginning to rise above the horizon and cast a pale golden glow on the mesquite trees surrounding the large tank, which livestock ponds of water are frequently called in Texas.

"Granddad, can I really shoot a duck with my .410?" I loudly whispered to him. "Yes, if they land close enough. But we have to be very still and quiet until they get here." He softly replied. We had gone to the tank the day before and built a blind made of large tumbleweeds that were trapped in a nearby barbed wire fence. My grandfather had brought three wooden milk crates, which he placed together in the center of the blind. He folded a wool army blanket over the top as padding for the seat and then set out the decoys.

We were staying in an old red brick hotel across the street from the large town square and courthouse in Graham, Texas. He frequently stayed there and used it as a temporary headquarters, while his tool pushers, derrickmen, roughnecks, and roustabouts drilled for oil on the ranch where we were now hunting ducks. The dimly lit lobby, furnished in dark brown leather wingback chairs and threadbare green brocaded sofas, smelled of stale cigar and cigarette smoke along with St. John's Bay Rum and Old Spice aftershave lotion, which was coming from the attached barbershop.

A long narrow glass-walled room, located in the lobby corner, sold cigars, cigarettes, magazines, candy and comic books, which I checked daily to see if a new "Superman" had arrived! Next to it was a shoeshine stand, which had two shoeshine "boys" busily working on hotel patron's cowboy boots and wingtip shoes. Watching them, I was mesmerized with their soft humming and the sound and rhythm of their shoe buffing rag, which snapped and popped loudly.

Men in khaki pants and boots, wearing sweat-stained gray Stetsons or dark brown fedoras, were sitting reading the Fort Worth Star Telegram's rig report or the oil well drilling news the paper contained. Several were "cutting deals" as they sat close together and spoke in hushed voices to prevent anyone from hearing the details. Graham was the county seat of Young County and the hub of activity for the oil industry in the region.

My grandfather was born in 1895 in Paul's Valley, Oklahoma six years after the state land rush had taken place. In 1911, at the age of sixteen, he left the family farm, after attending a one-room schoolhouse for eight years. Walking one hundred twenty-seven miles to Wichita Falls, Texas in Archer County, he went to work for a fledgling oil company there. He remained active in the oil business for the next fifty years ultimately owning several oil production companies and drilling rig operations.

"Quack…quack…quack…quack" my grandfather started blowing on the duck call after seeing a small flock flying towards the tank where we were hidden in the blind. "I want you to stand up now slowly, and I'll get your .410 ready to shoot." He whispered to me. I stood up, put my arms around the small shotgun, and got ready to shoot at a duck if one landed in the decoys about fifteen yards away. I had fired the Stevens single barrel shotgun several times before, and although my arms were not long enough to reach the trigger, I could tuck the stock under my right arm and fire it. I was not strong enough to cock the hammer, so my grandfather did. He called to the ducks several more times, and they came to the decoys near the shoreline.

Setting their wings; they swiftly glided in and landed with a splash. Granddad said, "Be very still." I did as he told me, then he whispered: "Shoot the closest one." I aimed down the barrel, put the front bead on the closest bird and pulled the trigger. The gun went off. "Bang" Immediately, the birds began to fly, except for the one I had shot and it was slowly flapping its wings while lying next to a wooden decoy, which I had also hit. "I hit it! I hit it! I hit it!" I yelled with glee while jumping up and down. My grandfather took the shotgun from me, opened it and removed the spent shell, replacing it with a fresh one. "Let's see if they will come back." He said. We watched the birds fly away, circle the tank, then leave. "Can we go get it now, Granddad?" After a few minutes, we moved away from the blind, and he waded in his rubber boots out into the shallow water, to the now dead bird and brought it back to the blind. It was a mallard drake with an iridescent green head and several curled feathers on its tail.

My grandfather was broadly smiling when he handed it to me. Taking the wet dead bird from his hands, I held it up to admire its color; then hugged it tightly saying, "Can I keep it until we go home so that I can show it to momma and grandmother?" My grandfather laughed and said, "No, we can't do that; however, we can take it to the hotel diner, and they will cook it for our supper tonight." "Now let's go back to the blind and see if any more will come in." I was shivering from the cold wind and holding the wet duck.

We went back to the blind, and as he picked me up putting me on his lap, he took the duck from my hands saying, "I'm really proud of you. This is the first of many of God's creatures you will harvest. But remember; never kill anything that you don't intend to eat unless it's a varmint or some other critter not worth eating." Beaming with pride and grinning widely I gleefully replied. "Yes, sir."

We sat there, but no other ducks came in, and after a while, we packed up and went back to the hotel. Driving to town, I fell asleep, sitting up, and my grandfather moved me over on the car bench seat so that my head was resting on his thigh. As his hand lay on my shoulder, all was well in my world, and I was happy and content. I imagine he was too.

When we arrived at the hotel, my grandfather woke me, and then he carried the mallard duck and the shot up decoy into the lobby with me sleepily following along. He stopped by the diner, spoke to the man behind the counter and left the dead duck with him. Taking my hand, we walked over to the elevator. Smiling down at me, he said, "Since you've shot the decoy, I'll tie a string around its neck, and you can play with it."

When we got to the room, he rummaged through a fishing tackle box until he found some braided cord. Taking out his pocketknife, he cut a length of it and tied it around the neck of the decoy. Handing it to me, he said, "Here you are, Son, your first trophy!" I took it from him, set it on the wooden floor and proceeded to walk around the room dragging it behind me. There were no other children at the hotel, so several "old" men, who knew my grandfather, teased me whenever I wandered around the lobby pulling the duck behind me. Within a few weeks, most of the paint had been worn off the decoy, but I did not mind, it was my "trophy," and I pulled it everywhere we went.

That evening the cook at the diner prepared the duck for us, and it was delicious served with mashed potatoes, green beans, and corn. Now I was officially a hunter! I have been on many duck hunts since then, but I have never forgotten how thrilled and excited I felt as a little boy shooting my first duck and how much I loved my grandfather.

Chapter Two

SETTLING IN

FINISHING MY COFFEE, I WALKED back to the truck and drove down the dry caliche road to the ranch headquarters. Off to the north, the dark clouds were rolling in with snow showers on the leading edge. It was going to get very cold tonight, which meant the deer hunting probably would be good the next morning.

Arriving at the cabin, I decided to check my rifle to see if it was still sighted in for three hundred yards. Many times, I had killed deer in West Texas at three hundred to four hundred yards away. I removed the gun from its case, laid it on top of my hunting parka that I had spread out on top of the warm truck hood. I was shooting a Sako Model 85 Bavarian in 7mm Remington Magnum caliber. It was a new rifle I had recently bought, after retiring my old Remington Model 700 BDL, which was of the same caliber. I had purchased that gun in 1964 in Lubbock while attending Texas Technological College; later renamed Texas Tech University. At the time, all my friends used either Winchester 30-30's, Remington 30-06's or 270's and many told me that I had made a dumb mistake buying an "oddball" caliber because no one would ever use a 7mm magnum and the cartridges would not be readily available. Of course, they were wrong, and for many years, it was the favorite rifle cartridge for most long-range shooters and hunters. In 1970, a Navy petty officer won the Camp Perry one thousand yard competition using one.

A few weeks earlier, I had installed a 30mm tubed, Swarovski Z6 scope in 2.5 to 15 power on the gun. It had an illuminated 4-plex reticle, side parallax knob, and a 56mm objective lens, so it was very good in low light environments. At $3,900, it cost nearly twice as much as the gun; but was one of the brightest and finest scopes in the world.

Carrying a full soda can about three hundred long paces down the dirt road next to the house, I placed it on its side in the crook of a mesquite tree at eye level. Only the silver bottom was showing, so my target was about two and a half inches in diameter. Back at the truck, I took out my Leupold range finder and measured the distance to the tree at 340 yards. I was shooting Hornady 162 grain SST® ("Super Shock Tip") Super performance® cartridges that had excellent ballistics of 3,030 feet per second muzzle velocity and 2,933 ft-lbs of energy. The scope was sighted in for the bullet to hit 3.5 inches high at one hundred yards, which put it dead on at three hundred yards.

I loaded one round in the chamber, put the safety on and set the scope to fifteen power. Turning my cap around backward, I stretched out against the warm truck hood, adjusted the parallax knob until the sight picture was crisp and clear, then moved the gun until it was firmly set in my coat. Placing the crosshairs on the silver can, I took a deep breath, let half of it out and slowly squeezed the two-pound trigger with the tip of my right index finger. "Boom" went the gun, and instantly the soda can exploded, spraying dark liquid in the air. "Well, that will work," I remarked to myself while opening the bolt, removing the spent brass and pocketing it.

Walking down to the mesquite tree, I found the can with one side blown out. The bullet had entered the bottom about a half inch above the center. "That'll put "El Viejo" down for sure," I said aloud while putting the gun back in its case and setting it on the back seat of the truck.

Long ago, I had learned not to bring a gun with a rifle scope into a warm house overnight and then take it outside the next morning, where the temperature was significantly colder. Condensation would form on the outside lenses causing difficulty in looking through the scope for a while.

Once inside the cabin, I built a fire in the fireplace, turned on the kitchen oven and then put a large pot of my "roadkill red" chili, I had previously made, on the stove. While it was warming, I mixed up a "pone" of buttermilk cornbread then put it in the heated oven. Twenty minutes later the chili was simmering, the cornbread was golden brown and it "sure smelled well" as my father-in-law Roy Gates used to say jokingly. Taking it out of the oven, I cut it into six pieces then "slathered" it with Kerrygold™ Irish butter, which I had brought with me.

I prepared a large bowl of chili, topped with chopped onions and covered with grated Mexican cheese. Putting two slices of cornbread on a paper plate, I carried everything to the kitchen table, sat down, bowed my head and prayed. "Dear Lord, thank you for all the blessings you've given me; especially my family and my wife, Peggy. I know she is opposed to me killing animals, but please let her continue to find it a "tolerable" character flaw she can occasionally overlook. Also, watch over me as I hunt and do not let me do anything dumb, like falling off an icy deer stand ladder. Amen."

Slowly, I began to eat, and the hot food was "Muy sabor agradable y delicoso."(Spanish: "Very tasty and delicious.") Suddenly, the wind began to howl outside, and sleet pelted the cabin's metal roof. The "blue northern" had arrived. As I ate, the intensity of the blowing wind increased and the sleet beat loudly.

"*Hombre,*" a good time will be had by all, tomorrow." I murmured laughingly to myself. I was glad that I had brought my cold weather hunting clothes and boots; most of which were rated for temperatures down to minus thirty degrees below zero. I was going to need it for sure.

After finishing supper, I put everything away, poured myself another Dr. Pepper and moved over to the rocking chair by the fireplace. Adding a couple of fresh logs, I stoked the fire and then sat down, smiling as I remembered that I once told a friend, with whom I was hunting, "different stokes for different folks" after he got up to stoke the fire right after I already had. The wind was still blowing very hard, but the sleet had stopped. Slowly rocking, I sipped my drink and gazed into the brightly glowing coals and flames. The crackling of the fire was peaceful sounding and very relaxing. Occasionally, I smelled the sweet mesquite smoke coming from the fireplace. I leaned back in the chair, closed my eyes and began to think about the first time I hunted quail with my grandfather.

FIRST QUAIL HUNT

"GRANDDAD, I SEE THEM," I said excitedly as we slowly walked down a dusty two-track dirt road on a ranch near Sweetwater, Texas. My grandfather's oil company crew had started clearing the mesquite trees with a bulldozer on a site where they planned to set up a drilling platform, rig, and derrick. The equipment would arrive in a few days; but until then, he and I were hunting quail for a few hours each day. "Son, stay beside me and be quiet so that they don't fly." He said. I waited for him to catch up to me and then I fell in step on the dirt track next to him. "If we can get close enough to the covey of "bobwhite" quail, I'll give you your .410 shotgun, and you can shoot one." He quietly said. "Is it okay if I shoot one on the ground?" I asked. "Yes, it is until you learn how to hit them on the fly. Then you will only want to shoot the ones flying." He answered. I thought "Hmm. How will I ever be able to kill a flying bird? A few years later, I could hit everything flying, if it was in the range of my gun.

In 1999, I was hunting quail on a friend's ranch near Crosbyton, Texas with my eighty-three-year-old father-in-law Roy B. Gates, who was from Monroe, Louisiana. When a large covey of bobwhite quail walked out of some empty cattle pens, we were approaching; I quietly asked, "Roy, do you shoot quail on the ground?"

With absolutely no hesitation at all, he laughingly whispered, "Do you mean they can fly?" We both then "cut down" on the covey with our twelve gauge shotguns and killed eleven birds with six shots. They sure were good for supper that night; fried golden brown with mashed potatoes, cream gravy, biscuits, and corn. *"Makes me hungry just writing about it."*

The bobwhite quail is the most abundant quail in Texas. The easily recognized "poor-bob-white" whistle of the male is heard during the spring and summer over most of the state. Quail populations have declined dramatically in the past decades primarily because of a loss of habitat and the invasion of "fire ants." Usually found in coveys of ten to twenty birds, bobwhite quail will all "flush" at the same time and fly a short distance away when sensing danger or startled.

The scaled quail, also known as the "blue" quail, is the second most prolific quail species. Having a large range, covering the majority of the western half of Texas, these birds are found in six of the eleven natural ecosystems of the state. They prefer a more arid climate and usually are not found where abundant rainfall occurs, like East Texas. Unlike bobwhite's, scaled quail usually inhabit dry areas that can sometimes average only four to six inches of rain per year. These quail usually are in coveys of a dozen to two dozen birds and their main defense when startled is immediately to scatter and run; not to "flush" as bobwhites do. Usually chasing them is futile unless you are on four wheelers, jeeps or horseback.

My grandfather and I were hunting bobwhite quail, which tend to stay in coveys and do not run very much. As we walked along, a mother bobwhite crossed the dirt road twenty yards ahead followed closely behind by six tiny mottled colored chicks that were no more than two inches tall. "Look, Granddad, there's one," I whispered. "I know. I see her, but we are not going to shoot because she has babies.

There are more up ahead, so in a minute let's walk slowly down the road." He quietly responded.

As we stood watching her, suddenly several more quail walked out into the dirt tracks, stopped and began to preen their feathers with their bills and rub their bellies in the soft dust. "Granddad, what are they doing? I whispered. "They are bathing in the dust to remove parasites and marking their territory." He softly said. Then my grandfather cocked my single barrel shotgun and slowly handed it to me saying "Son, shoot into the middle of the birds." I tucked the gun under my right arm, looked down the barrel, put the front bead on a middle bird and pulled the trigger. When the gun went off, dust flew up in the road, and two quail began wildly flapping their wings, while lying on the ground, as the rest of the covey flew off. Handing the shotgun to him, I excitedly said, "Look, Granddad, I got two" as I ran to pick them up. At first, I was afraid to touch them up because of their vigorous movements, but they soon stopped, and I reached down and picked them up by their feet.

The little .410 had not damaged the feathers much, even though I was shooting three-inch shells in #7.5's with 11/16th ounces of shot containing 241 pellets. My grandfather ejected the spent round and loaded a new one, then closed the action. "Son, you're doing really well. Soon you'll make a dog." He laughingly said. "A dog?" I asked, looking up at him. "When a bird dog learns to hunt and point and does well, it goes from being a pup to a making a dog." He explained as he smiled down at me. I thought about that for a minute then said: "Then I want to make a dog as soon as I can." I said and smiled. "You will I'm sure of it." He remarked.

Putting the two quail in the game pouch of his brown hunting jacket, he said. "Let's go find the rest of the covey and see if we can get some more. We need about a dozen so that we can have enough for supper for your mother, little sister, and Grandmother along with the two of us. But before we leave, let's eat a field lunch."

After taking a short break and eating cold canned Vienna sausages with saltine crackers and a cut up purple onion, we spent the afternoon hunting for more quail. They were "skittish" from being shot at, and only my grandfather could hit them with his twelve-gauge Winchester Model 12 pump shotgun, which had a modified choke Cutts Compensator on the twenty-eight-inch barrel. He was an excellent shot, and after finding other coveys, we had enough for supper.

I decided that day I was going to "make a dog" as fast as possible and ultimately I did. By the age of twelve, I was a better marksman with a shotgun than all of the men in my family, frequently breaking twenty-five or fifty clay birds straight in skeet or trap at the local gun range with my own Winchester model 12 shotgun. Somehow, the leads on moving targets were easy for me to pick up and learn.

Darrell Royal, the legendary head football coach of the University of Texas Longhorns, once said in his folksy twang, "It ain't bragging if you can do it." I'm not as good as I once was; but can still hold my own in Skeet, Trap and Sporting Clay tournaments.

CHAPTER THREE

TRACKS IN THE SNOW

AT 5:00 A.M., THE ALARM on my cell phone woke me. I went into the den and built a fire in the fireplace. After making coffee, I started dressing in layers, beginning with a set of expedition weight Capilene pants, shirt and then insulated jeans. Putting on Thinsulate boot socks and my Danner -30 degree rated insulated boots; I left off the insulated vest and shirt to keep from "sweating" out while eating an apple and cherry fried pie and drinking my coffee sitting by the fireplace.

I planned to leave at 5:45 a.m. and drive about three miles to a food plot, and electric game feeder near the river where "El Viejo" had recently been seen. After drinking my second cup of coffee, I went to the back door, pressed the remote starter on my keychain, and started my truck. I finished dressing, pushed the glowing embers to the back of the firebox and set the screen in front of the fireplace. Then I walked outside.

The temperature on the thermometer, hanging beside the door, read ten degrees. The wind was blowing fifteen to twenty miles per hour, which meant the "wind chill" was minus nine to minus eleven degrees. "Hombre, hace muy frio." (Spanish: "Man, it is very cold.") I said to myself as I walked to the truck. There were sleet and snow pellets on the windshield, so I waited until the defroster was blowing warm air before I drove away. I planned to go to the food plot and feeder, then park and slowly walk up to it. The day before I had tied some orange reflective tape to a mesquite limb, next to the caliche road, that marked the place for me to park one-half mile from the food plot.

As I slowly drove along, light snow was falling in front of the headlights. "Hmm." I thought. "That should help with any tracks I find on the ground and may tell me which direction the deer are traveling as they move into the food plot."

I suddenly saw the bright orange tape in front of the truck and slowly rolled to a stop next to it. I turned the headlights off to allow my night vision to recover and then switched off the engine. When I purchased the truck a year earlier, I took it to an electronics shop and had the remote starter added and a dash switch installed which allowed me to turn off all the interior and exterior lights when I opened the door. Sitting in the dark, I waited until the sky began to pale at first light. Soon, I started to see the mesquite trees and cedar bushes around me and slowly opened the door and got out, carrying my rifle. After quietly shutting the door, I loaded three 7mm magnum shells into the magazine, then slipped one in the chamber, closed the bolt and put on the safety. In all the years, since I first killed a deer in 1964, with the big magnum, I never had to shoot more than once. With superlative sectional density, excellent ballistic coefficient, and massive hydrostatic shock, one-shot kills were routine for the .284 diameter bullet. Roy B. Gates, my father-in-law, had used a 7mm Remington magnum since 1968.

Once, after he killed a trophy ten-point buck on his North Louisiana "Ten Mile Creek" lease, a friend asked him how far the deer went after he shot it. With a wry smile on his face, his reply was, "Three feet - straight down."

There was a light dusting of snow on the ground as I slowly walked along. Up ahead the dimly lit open field was coming into view and next to the road, stood the elevated, enclosed deer stand. I quietly walked over to it and noticed there was ice built up on the ladder rungs. Remembering my prayer from the night before, I slung the rifle across my back; carefully climbed the ladder and silently opened the door and stepped inside. All the windows were closed, so I turned on my small Stream light flashlight with a red lens, took my rifle off my back and propped it in the corner. I opened the blackout curtains, leaving the transparent Plexiglas sliders closed, which blocked the wind, but allowed me to see everything outside the stand.

The sky was beginning to lighten, and I could now see the five-acre food plot with the electronic game feeder thirty yards in front of the deer stand. Sitting down in the cushioned office chair, which swiveled and allowed me a 360° field of view, I took my Leica 8x32 binoculars from my parka and set them on the narrow shelf in front of me. After looking at my watch, I saw it was 6:15 a.m. Soon it would be legal for me to shoot, if "El Viejo" walked out.

Fifteen minutes later, the game feeder went off with a loud whirring noise, scattering whole kernel corn, and milo grain in a large circle around the three tall legs. Within two minutes, several turkeys began gobbling. Coming out from behind a large cedar bush, two large whitetail doe, one with a yearling, following closely behind, quickly walked to the feeder and began to eat the corn. "The food bell has rung, and breakfast is served." I laughingly thought to myself.

At the edge of the field, to my left, a flock of turkeys slowly walked to the feeder. The adult males were in front, and periodically would stop and fan-out their tail feathers and drop their wings down to ground level, hopefully impressing any females nearby that were not part of their harem.

The young males, called "jakes," were running willy-nilly behind them acting like goofy, playful, teenagers. The adult females were slowly strutting along, looking very majestic and frequently stopping to raise their heads and look around for any sign of danger. When they reached the feeder, they began to eat, but several kept a careful vigilance making sure no predators were nearby.

These turkeys were the Rio Grande species commonly found in most of South, Central and West Texas. Unlike a domestic Thanksgiving "butterball" turkey, which is plump and fat, these birds are tall, lean, long-legged and can run very fast. Their feathers have a greenish and black sheen. At night, the entire flock roosts in large trees, usually near a source of water.

As the sun peeked above the horizon, two sets of deer tracks became visible with both coming from the river and leading to the feeder. They were made after it snowed and sleeted during the night, which told me the two deer had been to the feeder earlier that morning. After a few minutes, a spike buck came out of the brush and walked to where the doe was grazing. Then, a six-point buck stepped out into the field and headed to the small group of deer.

It was a young healthy animal, probably no more than two and a half years old. Approaching the feeder, he grunted, lowered his head and ran off the spike buck. After a few moments, he began to eat the corn. Suddenly, he raised his head and looked back into the brush, nervously twitching his white tail. Then, a large mature ten-point buck stepped out from behind a big mesquite tree and began walking in the direction of the feeder. I thought, "Hmm, this is going to be interesting to watch."

As the buck stopped near the feeder, he raised his head, sniffed the air and curled its upper lip back trying to pick up any scent of estrus coming from the doe. Grunting loudly, he stomped his front legs, obviously challenging the other buck. Then, almost prancing, he walked to the feeder. As he got closer to it, the younger deer turned, flashed its white tail and ran away. The "rut" had occurred six weeks earlier, and both doe probably had mated and were pregnant. The larger buck quickly lost interest in them as he approached the feeder and began to eat the corn.

The sun slowly rose above a nearby hill to the east. While sitting there, bobwhite quail began to call to each other, "poor-bob-white." A covey flew out of the brush and landed near the game feeder. Then I understood why my friend had mixed milo in with the whole kernel corn; to feed the quail! Thinking, "That's smart. Now the quail will stay in the general vicinity of the feeder knowing that it's going off in the morning and again before dark, so they'll be fed twice a day." I had brought my Beretta 391 semi-automatic shotgun with me and decided that in a few days I would kill a "mess" of quail and cook them for supper.

There were deer, turkey, and quail all feeding together thirty yards in front of me. After about an hour, the birds and the deer had wandered back into the brush. I decided that I would spend the rest of the day sitting in the deer stand; to see if anything else, especially El Viejo, showed up. Leaning back in the comfortable chair, I began to think about the first time I ever hunted deer, sixty years earlier. As the memories flooded again, I felt a twinge of sadness and nostalgia because everyone about whom I now thought was long dead.

1952

THANKSGIVING MORNING

AFTER I PULLED THE TRIGGER on the Winchester Model 94, 30-30 lever action rifle, the whitetail doe, at which I was aiming, jumped, kicked her hind legs in the air and ran into the nearby dense mesquite brush. I started to get up, but my uncle "Mac" put his hand on my shoulder and quietly said to me, "No, let's sit here for a few minutes and then we'll go find her. The bullet hit just behind the front right leg, so it won't take long for her to die, but we need to wait a few minutes." He, my father and I were sitting in a dry cement-watering tank near a windmill. It was early Thanksgiving Day morning, and we were deer hunting on the McEntire "U" ranch which "Mac" and his father Fowler McEntire owned.

Two years before, my grandparent's youngest daughter, Sally Ann Heath, married Ewing F. "Mac" McEntire. They met at Texas Technological College where they were attending school. Mac had returned from World War II in 1946, after serving in the US Army in the Pacific Theater for three years as an infantry sergeant. He graduated from college, married my aunt, and they moved into a ranch house eight miles west of Sterling City, which is located forty miles Northwest of San Angelo, Texas on Highway 87.

I met uncle Mac when he married my Aunt Sally and liked him immediately, although he frequently smelled of chewing tobacco and spit a lot. As a young teenager, I once tried a "chaw" of tobacco he reluctantly gave me and about ten minutes later spit it out, after turning a shade of pale green and throwing up. That was the only time I ever used tobacco in any form. Mac taught me a lesson that lasted a lifetime.

He was a real "cowboy" that looked and dressed the part, with his faded jeans, dust-covered black Stetson hat and black pointed toe boots, called "roach killers" because they reached in corners. He also was the "spitting" image of the famous actor Robert Mitchum. Yes, Pun intended!

My dad, mother, little sister Penny and I had arrived at the ranch house the day before, after driving in from Austin, Texas. We had moved there earlier in the summer when my dad returned home from the Korean War. My mother was teaching elementary school at Wooldridge Elementary, where I went to first grade. My dad was completing his college education at the University of Texas and had a night job with the Austin Police Department as a radio dispatcher.

When we arrived the afternoon before, Mac asked if we would like to go deer hunting, the next morning and of course, the answer, from me, was a resounding "Yes." Later in the afternoon he, along with my father and I, took his 30-30 caliber saddle rifle and went out behind the barn, where there was open pasture. He set up several old rusted tin cans on a mesquite log about twenty yards away. Then he had me sit on the bare ground behind a short, weatherworn stump and showed me how to work the lever action, chamber a round and carefully lower the hammer to half cock.

Laying the fore end of the gun on the stump, he told me to line up the front bead in the "V" of the semi-buckhorn rear sight and shoot at one of the tin cans. I was wearing a leather jacket over a sweater, and Mac told me the recoil was not going to be too bad because of my thick clothing. He pulled the rifle stock tightly back into my shoulder, cocked the hammer and said, "Shoot!" Sighting down the barrel, I pulled the trigger, the rifle went off with a loud "bang" and the can, at which I was aiming, flew up in the air. The recoil was more than my .410 shotgun, but not so bad, that it hurt; although my ears were ringing from the report.

"Can I shoot again? I asked. "You sure can." He said while smiling down at me. I worked the lever action, chambered another round and placed the fore end on the stump. Pulling the stock tight against my shoulder, I said: "Let me do it all by myself." Lining the sights up on the remaining can, I pulled the trigger, and it flew back behind the mesquite log. Mac said, "I think you're ready for a deer if we see any." My dad, who had never seen me shoot, was smiling broadly and beaming with pride. When we left the pasture, he picked me up, put me on his shoulders and we walked back to the house. I was a happy camper and definitely enjoyed the company of men.

Until the mid-1960s, the deer population was decimated, almost to extinction, by the "screwworm" fly infestation that had ravaged the Southwest's population of cattle, sheep and whitetail deer since 1935. The screwworm fly is about twice the size of a housefly. It feeds, and lays its eggs, on bloody, open wounds and soft tissue of animals. The eggs hatch and then the larva (maggots) feed on the flesh, keeping the injury open and subject to further decay and infection.

The flies were attracted to a wound as small as a tick bite, so most wild animals, pets, and livestock were susceptible. Virtually all farm and ranch animals, including deer, giving birth, were destined to be infected with screwworms.

Fortunately, researchers in Kerrville, Texas, found that if the pupa were irradiated with radioactive isotopes, they could be made sterile and when the female screwworm fly mated with the sterile male no eggs would be produced and the population of flies would be eliminated.

In 1962, the program to eradicate the flies began by initially distributing nine hundred million sterile flies, released from airplanes, over vast areas of open West Texas ranchland. By 1966, the United States Department of Agriculture (USDA) declared screwworms completely eradicated. One consequence of this effort, other than the prevention of hundreds of millions of dollars in losses to Texas ranchers, was the effect the program had on the whitetail deer population.

It has been said that the screwworm fly was the last remaining efficient natural predator, other than man, for the deer in Texas. The elimination of the screwworm fly corresponds to the beginning of the largest increase in deer herd populations since records began to be kept in the late 1800's.[2]

Mac said, "Enough time's gone by now that the doe is down, so let's go find her." I jumped up and crawled over the cement side of the dry tank; waiting for Mac and my dad. We walked over to the area where the doe had been standing when I shot her. The ground was hard dirt and caliche and bare of any vegetation. Slowly, stepping over to where she had run into the dense mesquite, Mac stopped, squatted down and said, "Here's some blood. So she's probably not far away."

He got up and started walking further into the brush with my dad and me following closely behind. After a few minutes, he looked up and said, "There she is on the ground." He continued walking for a few steps until he was next to the doe. "You made a good shot." He told me, as he knelt down next to the deer.

I walked up to the doe and could see her white belly and tail as she lay on the ground and an entry wound behind her right shoulder. "Now the real work begins as we field dress her," Mac said. "But first

I need to do something." Reaching over to the entry wound, he stuck his right index finger into the bloody opening. "Come here Stan, Jr.," he said to me. I walked over to where he was squatted, and he took his bloody finger and made a vertical mark on my forehead between my eyes. "Now, you're a real deer hunter, for sure." He said while laughing. I smiled and vowed to myself never to wash my face, ever again.

Of course, my mother had a different opinion when I sat down at the Thanksgiving dinner table later that afternoon, still wearing what I considered my "red badge of honor." Coming over to me, with a Kleenex in her right hand, she spit on it, held my chin in her left hand and wiped the dried blood off my forehead. I started to protest, but knew it was useless after she gave me "the look." *(Longtime schoolteachers know how to do that very well!)*

Mac stood up, reached into his jeans and pulled out his pocketknife. Opening it, he said, "Let's roll her on her back, and I'll show you how to field dress a deer without ever getting any blood on your hands." He then proceeded to take the long, thin, razor sharp blade and make one cut, through the fur and skin, from the doe's chin, over the sternum, and belly to her anus. He was careful not to pierce the stomach. After cutting through the cartilage on her chest, he severed the windpipe, grabbed it with two fingers and told us to lay the deer on her side, but hold the legs apart. Then he began to pull, cutting all the connective tissue away from the spine as the entrails fell away from the internal cavity.

Once everything was pulled out, he made a circular cutting movement around the rectum and pulled the bladder and lower intestine away from the pelvis. The only blood on his hands was on his right index finger where he had marked my forehead. "That's how it's done, muchachos!" He said. "Uncle Mac, what is a muchachos?" I asked. He looked at me and said, "That is the Spanish word for boys." "I want to learn to speak Spanish. Can you teach me?" I asked. "Sure. However, it takes a long time to become fluent in the language. I've been speaking it all my life to the vaqueros Mexicanos that work on the ranch." He replied.

"What does vaqueros Mexicanos mean?" I asked. He laughed and said "Son, you sure do ask a lot of questions. We will work on your Spanish later. Let's head to the "Casa" and don't ask me what that means." Then he tousled my hair saying. "Vamanos!" I grinned at him and knew we were going to be lifelong friends. And we were until he was accidentally killed in 1976 after a horse he was riding during a cattle roundup, fell on him.

Loading the doe in the back of his 1948 F-1 Ford pickup, we drove to the house. My grandparents (the Heaths) had just arrived from Colorado City, and everybody was outside greeting them. When my dad opened the truck door, I jumped out and ran over to my grandfather saying "Come look at the deer I shot, Granddad!" as I grabbed his hand and excitedly pulled him along.

Everyone walked over to the bed of the pickup and looked at the dead deer. My mother made a sharp gasping noise, picked up my little sister and quickly walked to the house. My grandmother and Sally followed her. "The "womenfolk" are little squeamish about dead animals, but that's a fine looking deer and will make some tasty venison cuts and sausage," Granddad said.

While I watched the next morning; Mac and the "menfolk" skinned and cut up the deer; packaging the "backstrap" and various choice cuts of venison in white butcher paper. The remainder of the meat was mixed with pork, sage, and spices in a hand grinder made into sausage and put into several two-pound packages of butcher paper. Now, I was part of the "hunter clan" and remained so for the rest of my life.

Chapter Four

MORE TRACKS IN THE SNOW

AFTER EATING SOME LEFTOVER CORNBREAD and another apple-fried pie, I had brought with me from the house; I washed it down with a cold Dr. Pepper. Then I got up, slung my rifle over my back and carefully climbed down the deer stand ladder. I walked over to the two sets of tracks near the center of the food plot. Apparently, at some time there had been a lightning strike because there was an area approximately twenty feet in diameter in which all the vegetation had died. It was in this bare spot that I had seen the two sets of deer tracks in the snow. Kneeling down, I saw they were coming from the direction of the river. Both were made by large, mature deer whose weight had pressed the track down into the soft dirt leaving clear impressions of the dewclaws.

Hunters have long debated whether a deer's sex can be determined from its tracks. Many times the presence of dewclaws has erroneously been identified as a sign that the track maker was a buck. There are a number of factors that affect whether or not a dewclaw impression will be left, including the dryness and texture of the soil, whether the track came from a front or back hoof, and whether the deer was walking or running. Because of these factors, dewclaws in the track are not a reliable indicator of sex. Front hooves of an average adult whitetail buck will be about three inches long and one and one half to two inches wide. Additionally, the dewclaws on the front legs are closer to the hooves than the ones on the rear, which makes it quite easy to tell a rear foot from a front foot.

What many hunters have known all along is that a buck likely makes a bigger track, but it is impossible to tell the sex of an average size track based on its size alone. Despite the presence of tracks, there is only one sure way to be absolutely certain about the sex and size of the deer that made it and that is to find the track while the deer is still in it! [3]

Both tracks were large; however, one was bigger than the other was. "Could this be "El Viejo" and a large doe?" I wondered. However, the rut had already taken place several weeks earlier, and it was not likely that he was running with a doe and certainly, he would not be consorting with a smaller buck. While bucks will frequently gather in "bachelor" groups before the rut starts, once it begins, they all become loners and rivals. The big tracks were puzzling. I walked over to the electronic feeder and looked at all the tracks surrounding the base. There had been so much activity that morning by the turkey, quail and other deer that I could not see any large tracks.

After walking back to the deer stand, I slung my rifle over my back and climbed up into the interior. I sat there the rest of the afternoon, but only saw a coon, a skunk and a huge bright reddish orange fox that came sniffing around the feeder. I wished that I had brought my single shot .22 Hornet rifle with the 4x12-power Leopold scope to kill the fox and have a full-bodied mount done by a taxidermist I knew in Fort Worth. Shooting it with my 7mm magnum would do too much damage to the pelt. So, I watched the animal for a while and then it trotted back into the brush.

Thirty minutes before dark, the feeder went off, the turkeys, quail, and several doe returned and began eating the corn and milo.

However, not "El Viejo!" After dark, I packed up and walked back to my truck thinking, "Maybe tomorrow will be the day I harvest the "Old Man."

After entering the cabin I built another fire, undressed and put on a soft flannel shirt and well-worn jeans; then slipped into my shearling-lined deerskin moccasins. Warming the rest of the chili, I heated two slices of cornbread in the microwave and sat down at the kitchen table. Bowing my head, I said, "Lord, thank you for keeping me safe today, as you have for so many years in my life, especially when I was flying helicopters in Vietnam. I will always be eternally grateful for your grace and mercy. Amen."

After eating and washing the dishes, I sat down in the rocker in front of the fireplace. "What are we going to recall from the past?" I thought to myself. At first, nothing came to mind, and I sat there listening to the crackling fire and remembering the menagerie of animals and birds that came to the food plot and automatic feeder.

Then I thought about the flock of turkeys. "Caramba. Se me olvido los guajolotes!" (Spanish: "Good gracious. I forgot about the turkeys!") I said aloud. "What an adventure that was; hunting turkeys on the North Concho River for the first time, when I was nine years old." Starting to chuckle, I soon was laughing and wiping tears from my eyes recalling the hilarious episode.

My first turkey experience became a seminal event in my early development as a hunter, when I learned, the "hard way," that sometimes you just have to shut up, gut up, grin and bear it and "take" what's thrown your way. A few years later, the men in my family would proudly say, "That boy, sure enough, has grit!" I do not think they were talking about the sand in my ears and nose from once hunting prairie dogs one day during a major dust storm, which had appeared very suddenly, near the little town of Whiteface in West Texas. But, that is another story in a later chapter.

1954

CHRISTMAS BREAK

CRASH... CRACK... SNAP! WAS THE loud sound the flock of turkeys made as a dozen of them wildly flew through the tree limbs after having been awakened by a headlamp shined up in their midst. It was midnight, and they were roosting in a big pecan tree next to the river. My uncle Mac, his friend Delbert, who was leaving for the US Army the next day, and I were "coon" hunting late one night. It was a dark, clear, starry night and tranquil as we slowly walked along the riverbank looking in the trees for the bright reflective eyes of coons.

When Mac shined his headlamp up through the giant tree, suddenly the birds were "spooked," and all of them flew off at once. Hearing, but not seeing the turkeys, I immediately ducked and grabbed my head thinking the "thing in the woods" was finally attacking us. As they crashed through the tree, most of the turkeys had a cloacal evacuation, which meant that they "pooped" everywhere uncontrollably. Standing directly below them, we were suddenly covered in turkey crap.

Mac and Delbert started laughing aloud and slapping their knees. I stood there with warm smelly poop running down my head, neck and face; wanting to cry, but determined not to do so in front of the two men. Mac took out a red handkerchief, walked to the riverbank and dipped it in the water. Coming over to me, he said, "Here, use this to clean your head and face." Still shaking like a leaf, and with quivering lips, I took the wet handkerchief and cleaned the poop off as best I could and gave it back to him.

He washed off the handkerchief in the river and began to clean up. "At least now we'll know where to come to hunt turkeys tomorrow," Mac said with a laugh. With all the loud commotion of the panicked turkeys and the fact that we still had turkey poop on our clothes, we walked back to the pickup and went to the house.

The lights were on, and after going in the back door, I saw that my mother, Aunt Sally, and my grandparents were playing bridge and were looking down at their cards as I walked up to the table not saying anything. When my mother saw me standing beside her, she immediately shrank back and said, "What have you got all over your clothes and hair?" as she put her hand over her nose. About that time, Mac walked into the living room and said, "Howdy everyone. As you can see, and smell, Stan, Jr. and I had an up close and personal encounter with a flock of turkeys roosting in a pecan tree by the river." Everyone started laughing when he said that. My mother said, "We'll have to continue the game tomorrow." She turned to me and said, "Let's go to the bathroom and get you cleaned up and then to bed." My dad, who had worked five straight night shifts before we left Austin, came out of the bedroom yawning and rubbing his eyes. As we left the room, Mom looked back over her shoulder, said, "Boys will be boys, I suppose!" and started laughing, then pointed at my uncle, Mac. He smiled too.

The next morning Mac, my dad and I went back to the river where we had the "close encounter of the turkey kind." However, there were no turkeys there. Earlier in May, on my ninth birthday, I had been given a Savage Model 24, .22/.410 over and under rifle/shotgun and was holding it between my knees, while sitting in the back seat of a surplus WWII Willis, Jeep. Mac was driving, and my dad was sitting in the right seat. They both had 12 gauge shotguns; dad had his Winchester model 12 pump and Mac had a recently acquired L.C. Smith side-by-side double-barreled shotgun. Suddenly Mac slammed on the brakes and said, "There they are on the side of the mesa!" He took out some army surplus binoculars and looked at the flock for a few minutes. Saying, "I don't think we're going to be able to drive up close enough to them, to get a shot with the shotguns." Reaching into the rifle carrier attached to the folded down windshield, he removed a pre-war built Winchester Model 70 in .270 caliber rifle with a four-power K-4 Weaver scope attached. Mac handed the rifle to my dad and said, "When we get in close enough, try to shoot a couple of the "Tom's" with this. He was using Winchester 130-grain Silver Tip bullets that were very flat shooting. Slowly driving along, we got within one hundred yards of the turkeys, and the jeep rolled to a stop. My dad leaned forward and placed his left elbow on the dashboard. Shouldering the rifle, he looked through the scope and "snicked" off the safety. Then taking a deep breath, he fired, instantly ejecting and loading another shell. A "tom" in the front of the turkey flock, exploded with a big "poof" of flying feathers and the bird instantly dropped to the ground. The other birds milled around and then started running in our direction. Fifty yards away, they saw the jeep and stopped.

Dad, who had been looking through the scope, aimed at another male bird and fired. Another burst of feathers flew from a big turkey, and it began flopping on the ground as the others took flight and flew away. "Muchachos, that's the easy way to hunt turkeys!" Mac said. He drove over to the closest bird, and we all got out looking at the "tom." It had a six-inch long beard and was very healthy, except for the bullet hole in its chest, with dark black and bluish-green colored feathers.

Getting back in the jeep, we drove to the first bird. It was an even bigger male. Dad had hit it, just at the base of its neck. "Stan, where did you learn to shoot like that?" Mac asked. Dad said, "I grew up in southern Ohio and frequently would hunt squirrels with my dad along the Ohio River with my .22 caliber rifle. I got pretty good shooting them. Then, on our days off from flying, in Iwo Jima, we would take 30 caliber M-1 carbines and eight shot M1 Garand's, go into the hills next to the flight line, and shoot at J-A-P-A-N-E-S-E B-O-D-I-E-S; spelling the letters out. Sounding exasperated, I said, "Dad, I'm in the third grade and can spell, so I know what you just told Mac!" They both laughed, and Dad said, "Okay, but don't say anything to your mother." I said, "I won't." Suddenly, I realized I had just entered a man's world; where keeping certain things away from a woman was acceptable, and it felt really good. From that moment on, I did not want to have anything to do with other children, unless they were my younger sister or cousins.

We drove back to the house and unloaded the guns and the two dead turkeys. Turning to me, Mac said, "It's time you learned how to clean birds, so when I come back, I'll show you how. He and my dad went inside, and a few minutes later, they came out each carrying a water glass half-full of J.W. Dant bourbon whiskey and were sipping from them.

Mac showed me how to skin a turkey; not pluck it. It only took a few minutes, and once the "innards" were removed, we took the carcasses to a water faucet in the yard, washed the blood off, and cleaned our hands. Bringing them inside, he asked my Aunt Sally and my grandmother if they would cook the wild turkeys along with the butterball. At first they were a little reluctant, but finally said they would.

For Christmas dinner, we had both types of turkeys, and the wild ones were more flavorful but somewhat tough. Years of running from coyotes, varmints and roosting in trees made them that way.

CHAPTER FIVE

SEEING "EL VIEJO"

AT 5:30 A.M., AFTER EATING a breakfast of sausage, eggs, and biscuits, I dressed and remotely started my truck so it could warm up. Then I took four biscuits, cut them open, inserted a thick piece of sausage inside each, and tightly wrapped them in "tin foil" before placing them in one of the large pockets of my parka. Making sure the fire was banked, and the screen was in place, I walked out to the truck, opened the hood and set the sausage and biscuits on top of the idling engine. Years earlier, I had read about warming and cooking food placed on a truck engine. It really works.

As I neared the reflective tape and slowly rolled to a stop a huge deer stepped out into the road, thirty yards in front of the truck, stopped, turned and faced me. With two sizeable misshapen drop tines, one on each side of its horns, and so many gnarly points I could not count them all, I realized I was looking at "El Viejo!" His body was very heavy and much darker than any other whitetail deer I had ever seen or killed. Could this be a hybrid whitetail/mule deer or just a mule deer that had wandered far from its usual range in South Texas and stayed for so many years?

The big deer slowly raised its tail, indicating nervousness, but did not run away. I saw the tail was shorter than a whitetail's and was whitish with a big black tip; a definite sign of a mule deer. Also, its ears were much larger than the whitetail species. "El Viejo" was looking more and more like a true, but non-typical mule deer.

The two species tend to segregate themselves somewhat, as mule deer prefer rougher canyons and ravines; while the whitetails are more commonly found in brushy open pastures. The ranch had numerous deep senderos with lots of cedar brush in them, so in all likelihood "El Viejo" was bedding down there and only wandered out occasionally looking for food. The buck probably spent most of his time in the thick cedars in a non-descript location that made seeing him nearly impossible.

Its horns were very wide and tall with too many points going in multiple directions to count, from my vantage point sitting in the truck. Both main beams were very thick with dozens of small protrusions coming off them and were probably twenty-four inches in length. The inside spread was around eighteen to twenty inches. My predicament was how to get my rifle off the back seat, load it, open the door and get a shot at "El Viejo."

The problem was suddenly resolved when the massive deer whirled and ran back into the heavy brush. I realized that I had been holding my breath most of the time while watching the deer and could now feel my heart beating rapidly with a slight pain radiating up my throat. "Hmm." I thought. "I know what that feeling is, a precursor to a heart attack." I started taking deep breaths, then removed a tiny pill bottle out of my shirt pocket and swallowed one nitroglycerin tablet. Within two minutes, the pain subsided completely. I started to laugh as I thought, "It's been a long time since I've suffered from buck fever, but seeing "El Viejo" that close, sure enough, brought it on."

I knew I was not going to see him at the food plot now, so I decided to drive the interior roads and look for areas that a mule deer would likely stay. The ranch was three miles wide and fourteen miles long which meant that it was forty-two sections of land or twenty-six thousand eight hundred and eighty acres. It was small by West Texas ranching standards, but big enough that one deer, which was older and wiser, could easily stay concealed for years.

Before leaving for the hunt, I printed off topographic maps of the ranch that showed all of the roads, so I took them out and looked for deep ravines, senderos and canyons with roads nearby. I spent the next several hours driving to various locations that looked promising; however, I only saw several whitetail bucks which I jumped while driving across the open pastures. At 2:00 p.m., I pulled the truck up to the rim of a mesa overlooking a long narrow canyon and turned the engine off. Opening the hood, I took the hot biscuits and sausage from the top of the air cleaner, and while sitting inside the cab, I ate them. Afterward, I took out my binoculars and slowly began to look at the narrow canyon. It was isolated and densely covered in cedar bushes and large stands of poplar and cottonwood trees, a perfect place for an old "muley" to hide.

After an hour of watching for any movement, and not seeing any, I decided to go back to the ranch house. "I think I'll come back here tomorrow morning before sunrise and see if anything moves down in the canyon." Starting the engine, I marked my current location by placing a "waypoint" on the Garmin GPS. Slowly driving to the nearest road, I stopped and marked the route I had taken to the mesa on my topo map with a pencil. Then periodically I marked "waypoints" as I drove back to the house.

Changing clothes, I found a big black iron skillet in a kitchen cabinet and decided to pan-fry a thick rib eye steak, which I had brought with me. I cleaned an Idaho potato, popped it in the microwave sitting on the countertop, and began to bake it. Then taking out a pan, I heated water in it and made some whole kernel corn. Putting some Irish butter in the skillet and melting it over a hot gas flame, I cooked the steak to perfection, the way I like it; charred black on both sides and rare on the inside. After the potato was done, I drained the water off the corn, mixed some Philadelphia cream cheese with chives into it, and then took everything to the kitchen table. Buttering the hot baked potato, I lowered my head to pray. Then a fleeting thought flashed through my brain as I remembered hunting prairie dogs the summer after I had my misadventure with the roosting turkeys. "That's what I'll conjure up in a little while when I finish supper. After praying, I ate the steak, baked potato and corn then washed everything. Pouring my favorite "libation," I sat down in the rocker by the glowing fire, full and contented.

1955

PRAIRIE DOG HUNTING

"ARE YOU SURE YOU WANT to stay out here all day?" my grandfather asked as I got out of his car with my Savage .22/.410, an army surplus blanket, a sack lunch and metal army canteen inside a faded cloth carrier, attached to a well-worn web belt. "Yes, sir. I'll be okay." I said. Checking to make sure I had three boxes of .22 long rifle hollow points and a box of three-inch #6 .410 shotgun shells; I hooked the buckle on the web belt after putting it around my waist and put the other items in an olive drab green rucksack; which I slung over my shoulders.

I asked Granddad, "What time do you think Halliburton will be through with the hydraulic fracking of the well?" He replied. "They should be finished before dark. But in any event, I will pick you up by then. Just be on the road and remember; do not pick up any prairie dogs you shoot or find dead because sometimes they will have bubonic plague-infected fleas and that will kill you if you contract it. Be sure to stay away from any rats you see in the burrows because they carry diseases too." "I'll be careful Granddad," I said. "Also, watch out for rattlesnakes; they like to live in prairie dog holes, and since it's been so warm the past few weeks they'll be out today." He warned me.

As he drove away, I waved to him and began to walk about a mile to the center of a six thousand four hundred acre prairie dog "town." It was west of Whiteface, Texas; approximately eight miles east of the New Mexico state line. The site at which I was hunting was two miles wide and five miles long and contained hundreds of thousands of prairie dogs, all living close together in dirt mound burrows. The pasture had no vegetation or trees.

I was hunting the black-tailed prairie dog, which is a close cousin of the ground squirrel. They have large eyes, short tails with black tips and a brownish-tan pelt. The presence of a prairie dog town is devastating for landowners who need the pastures for cattle, sheep, hogs or other livestock. They dig extensive tunnels and burrows, creating deep holes. Livestock, especially cattle, frequently will step in them and break their legs, and then they must be euthanized costing the landowner thousands of dollars in losses. Additionally, prairie dogs carry fleas and diseases, such as the deadly "bubonic plague" and the rats living in the abandoned burrows frequently have "hantavirus" which can be passed on to humans. Eating the same grasses as the livestock means the prairie dogs are competing for the same natural resources as the rancher's primary income provider and jeopardizes his livelihood. In short, they are a nuisance, a pest and are undesirable in every location they inhabit.

Prairie dogs live as a group in prairie dog "towns." These towns are subdivided into wards that are arranged like counties within the state. Wards are further subdivided into distinct social units called "coteries." A coterie usually consists of a single adult male, one to four adult females and any offspring less than two years of age. Movement between wards is uncommon.

When prairie dogs are out, a sentry perches on the volcano-like ring that surrounds the burrow. Should a predator or any other danger become evident, the sentry will bark out a warning, after which the community will dive into their burrows and wait for the "all clear" call before venturing out again. In Texas, they are found in western portions of the state and the Panhandle. Huge prairie dog towns, such as one that covered 25,000 square miles and supporting a population of approximately 400 million prairie dogs, once were reported in West Texas.[4]

As I walked to the middle of the prairie dog town, thousands of them were scampering and running between their burrows and barking at me. On several occasions, Granddad and I had stopped along the dirt road running beside their "town," and he let me shoot at them with my .22 rifle. I could hit one on the first shot out to about seventy-five yards.

Reaching the middle of the pasture, I removed my rucksack, took the army blanket out and spread it on the hard ground. Then I took off my web belt with the canteen and sat down cross-legged facing the west. Every ten or fifteen yards there was a prairie dog mound; most with one sitting on top looking at me. For a while, I sat there quietly drinking a few sips of water. Then after opening my rucksack and removing a sandwich bag, I began to eat a homemade mincemeat fried pie that my grandmother had prepared for me. It was 8 o'clock in the morning, and a cool a gentle wind was blowing from the west. Sitting there, I decided to be very still and let everything settle down.

After thirty minutes, the prairie dogs ignored me and went about their business of "socializing" with each other. Quietly, opening the action of my gun, I loaded a .22 long rifle hollow point and a #6-shotgun shell into the chambers. Closing the action, I rested the gun on my raised left knee and sighted at a prairie dog sitting on top of a mound approximately thirty yards away. When I pulled the trigger, I heard a "thump" when the bullet hit the animal; however, it fell into the burrow. I stood up, walked over and looked down into the hole. There were blood droplets around the rim, but no sign of the prairie dog. I thought, "Granddad didn't have to worry about me touching a prairie dog, because I may never see what I've shot."

I put another .22 long rifle in the gun, sat down on the blanket, and looked around for another shot. Most of the nearby prairie dogs had dived into their burrows at the crack of the rifle. As I waited, a few began to stick their heads out of the holes. Soon, they all were sitting on top of their mounds, and several were running around between them. When one stopped running and rose up to look at me, I slowly raised my left knee, laid my gun on it, took careful aim and fired at it. Instantly, the hollow point hit its mark, and the prairie dog flipped over backward and lay still. I stood up and walked over to where the critter was laying. It was a lot bigger than a ground squirrel and much heavier. With my rough out leather boot toe, I rolled it over and saw that I had made a center mass shot. "This is going to be a lot of fun," I said aloud.

Throughout the morning, I continuously shot and hit targets, sometimes out to nearly one hundred yards. When the sun was directly above me, I opened my rucksack and took out a sandwich made with thick slices of roast beef, lettuce, and tomatoes, which my grandmother had made for me. Sitting there with a slight westerly wind blowing, I decided I always wanted to live in West Texas, and for many years, I did just that.

I wished that my dad were with me to see all the prairie dogs; however, in January the US Air Force had sent him to Japan. He was one of four American fighter pilots chosen to train Japanese Air Force pilots how to fly jet aircraft. The training was done in T-33 single-engine airplanes at Tsuiki Air Force Base. His first student was General Minoru Genda, who planned and carried out, the raid on Pearl Harbor on December 7, 1941.

Later, my dad said they became close friends, even though ten years earlier they were bitter enemies. After his training, General Genda became the commander of the Japanese Air Force and later was a politician in the Japanese government.

My mother, sister and I finished the school year in Austin and then moved to Levelland, Texas, where we lived with my grandparents who had moved there from Colorado City. My grandfather's oil company had obtained numerous leases in the Permian Basin near the New Mexico border, and so he had moved his whole operation further west to be closer to the drilling sites and oil fields, which were being established.

After eating, I gathered everything and moved closer to the road where my grandfather had dropped me off. Quietly sitting there, soon the prairie dogs began to come out of their burrows with many running between the holes. When one stopped about forty yards away, I shot it; got up and started walking over to where it lay. Suddenly I heard a loud buzzing noise coming from a yucca plant five feet away from where I was standing. Coiled next to it was a western diamondback rattlesnake furiously shaking its rattles at me. Slowly turning, I raised the rifle/shotgun to my shoulder and moved the barrel selector button down to fire the .410. The snake was huge and thick around the body. I shot its head off; opened the action, ejected the shotgun shell and replaced it with another. The snake's body was violently flopping around on the ground even though the head was missing.

I stood there a few minutes, then walked over to the slowly squirming body and picked it up by the tail. It began to thrash around and turned to bite me even though there was no head. Amazingly, its muscle memory was designed instinctively to strike at any potential danger.

The "vibora cascabel," which is Spanish for "vibrating snake" had seventeen rattles and was nearly seven feet long; when I held its body up over my head, and most of the tail still lay on the ground. As I turned to carry it back to the blanket, I heard another loud buzzing sound next to a yucca bush only three feet away. "Oh, my gosh, there's another snake." "Granddad was right about the snakes being out today." I thought. Setting the first snake on the ground, I fired at the second one's head, instantly killing it. The second rattlesnake started wildly flopping around on the ground, as the first one had done. Opening the action of my gun, I removed the spent shotgun shell and replaced it with a fresh one. Waiting a few minutes before going to look at the second snake, I wondered, "Why are there so many rattlesnakes here and there were none when I first set up earlier that morning?" I decided that as the day warmed up, the snakes came out of the abandoned burrows where they were living.

I picked up the first snake then walked over to the second one and picked it up by its tail. Taking them back to the blanket, I took out my pocketknife, which Granddad had sold to me for one penny saying, "Its bad luck to give a pocketknife to someone." And cut the rattles off and set them on a flat rock next to the blanket. The second snake had twelve rattles, and I thought, "Wow, it's a lot more fun to shoot snakes than prairie dogs because now I've got something to show for my efforts."

Many people believe that the number of rattles indicates its age; however, that is not true. As the snakes grow, they periodically need to shed their old skin to accommodate their larger body. When it is time, a shedding snake will try to snag a piece of their skin on a stick or rock and slither out of it.

Each time an old skin is shed, a new rattle is added. Younger snakes will shed their skin two or three times a year as they grow; whereas older ones will shed maybe only once a year. Rattlesnakes give live birth and can have up to twenty-five babies (called neonates) in a brood. Full-grown rattlesnakes can range from three to eight feet in length and weigh nearly ten pounds. The average rattlesnake lives fifteen to twenty years.

I started walking around looking for more snakes, but after an hour, and not seeing anymore, I returned to the blanket, sat down and waited for more prairie dogs to come out. The wind speed had picked up considerably and was steadily blowing from the Northwest. I shot several more prairie dogs as the afternoon progressed. The wind was increasing rapidly, and soon I began to see a vast, wall of brown sand hundreds of feet tall on the horizon; coming in my direction.

"Hmm, I better head back to the road and wait for Granddad." I thought. I wrapped the two rattlesnake rattles in the "tin foil" from my sandwich and put them in my knapsack along with the army blanket. By the time I got to the road, the wind was already blowing forty or fifty miles per hour, and the flying dirt was stinging my eyes and face.

The caliche road was recently graded, and there were several big white limestone rocks on the side, so I sat down on one, opened my rucksack and took out the blanket. Unloading my gun and laying it on my legs, I pulled the blanket over my head and turned my back to the approaching dust storm. Soon the sky darkened, and the visibility dropped to only a few feet. I could barely see the road, and nothing on the other side, as the wind velocity increased to seventy miles per hour; which is typical for most dust storms in West Texas.

"I sure hope Granddad gets here soon." I thought as the wind howled and buffeted me. Then I heard a car horn blowing from somewhere down the road. I sat huddled there waiting for him to come to me. Although I could not see it at first, his car slowly pulled up next to me, and he rolled the window down yelling, "Do you want to come home with me or sleep in one of the prairie dog holes?" I yelled back, "I think I'll go home with you because there are too many rattlesnakes out here. I killed two big ones just a little while ago." "You did what!" Granddad loudly said in surprise. "I killed two big rattlesnakes and cut their rattles off. They are in my rucksack. I'll show them to you when we get home." Opening the door, I slid my gun into the back seat floorboard, took off my army blanket and rucksack and set them beside it. After closing the door and sitting down in the passenger seat, I was glad to be out of the strong wind and dust storm. My hair was covered with sand, and it was in my ears and nose. Granddad smiled at me, and with tears in his eyes said, "Son you've just made a dog, that's for dang sure." I sat there and smiled at him while shaking the dirt out of my hair. I felt like I had just undergone, and passed, a survival ordeal and a rite of passage that I would always remember.

Chapter Six

CANYON SANCTUARY

WHILE THE BACON SIZZLED AND popped in the black cast-iron skillet, I put a cookie sheet filled with buttermilk biscuits in the heated oven. When the bacon was cooked, I removed it and put two tablespoons of flour in the grease. Taking a metal spatula and stirring the mixture together, "First you make a roux." I laughingly said aloud, thinking of my wife Peggy who is from Louisiana and a great cook of Cajun cuisine. The secret to making good smooth gravy is to be sure each grain of flour is saturated with grease. Then I added milk, salt, and pepper and let everything begin to simmer while stirring continuously for about twenty minutes.

Many years earlier, from 1974 to 1981, I had spent most of each November and December taking bankers, real estate developers and others, with whom I was doing business, to West Texas where I had a twenty-thousand-acre hunting lease. In addition to being the guide and outfitter, I also did all of the cooking, so I became very proficient in that aspect of the operation too. Once the biscuits were golden brown, I fried three eggs in a Teflon pan and then took everything to the kitchen table, sat down, bowed my head and prayed.

"Heavenly Father, I know the sands of time are running out for me, and I'm very grateful for each day that I have left on earth. Yesterday, the chest pain I experienced, upon seeing "El Viejo" for the first time, was a subtle reminder of how close I am to reaching my final destination with you. I am blessed beyond measure with a loving wife and family, and you have restored my wounded soul. Thank you. Amen."

After eating and cleaning up the kitchen, I remotely started my truck and made sure the fireplace was secure. I packed a lunch of bacon, biscuits and a couple of fried pies, then went to the truck and slowly began to drive in the direction of the senderos and shallow canyon ravine. I had a dash mounted, touch screen, Garmin Montana 680t GPS with built-in topographic maps and waypoint tracking capability. Turning it on, I pressed, "navigate" and touched the waypoint at the canyon. Instantly the device showed me the route back to it and the distance, which was approximately seven miles.

The previous evening, I had removed my Leupold 20x60 power tactical spotting scope, with an 80-millimeter objective lens, from its case and put it in the truck. I also made sure that I had the window glass mount with me too. I slowly followed the navigation route back to the canyon, arriving thirty minutes before sunrise. Turned the engine off, I toggled the dash switch that killed all the lights. Rolling the window partially down, I attached the spotting scope in the bracket and looked at the dark canyon through it. The scope's light-gathering capability was excellent because of the large objective lens; however, it was too dark to see anything. I poured a cup of coffee from my thermos and slowly sipped it while waiting for daylight and the legal shooting time of 6:30 a.m.

The shallow canyon was formed during the Cretaceous period at the time that Double Mountain Fork Brazos River and the two Double Mountain Buttes were created. Over the millennia, cedar bushes, poplar, and cottonwood trees had grown up and nearly filled the steep-sided ravine providing excellent cover and habitat for the deer and other wildlife living in the area.

Before the end of the Plains Indian Wars in 1875, Quanah Parker, the famous chief of the Comanche Indian tribe, and son of Cynthia Ann Parker had set up his camp near the canyon at the base of the buttes. For many years buffalo hunters roamed the area and used the two buttes as primary navigation points to pinpoint the buffaloes location; with scouts climbing to the mountain tops looking for huge herds of the animals in the vast plains area stretching out below.

It was from this camp at dawn on June 27, 1874, that Parker led seven hundred warriors, including many Kiowa, Cheyenne, and Arapaho, to the tiny Adobe Walls Fort, near the Canadian River and attacked twenty-eight buffalo hunters. Twenty-year-old William Barklay "Bat" Masterson was among the group and later became known as a fearless gunfighter, sheriff, saloonkeeper and finally New York City newspaper sports writer. The hunters' superior long-range weapons enabled them successfully to fend off the attackers.

One hunter, William "Billy" Dixon shot and killed a Comanche warrior sitting astride a horse at 1,538 yards using a borrowed Sharps Model 1874 rifle in .50-90 caliber. In the three-day battle, four buffalo hunters died. However, seventy Indians were shot and killed and many others, including Parker, were severely wounded before they retreated from the area. They were so disillusioned and discouraged with the killing of a warrior at such a long distance that they gave up the fight. Their failed attack ultimately led to the end of the conflict between the white settlers and the Plains Indians.

As the night sky faded, I began to see the ravine and flat pastures on either side. Looking through the powerful spotting scope, I could clearly make out several trails (senderos) leading into it. While watching; several whitetail doe and one mature buck, but not "El

Viejo" walked out of the canyon and headed in the direction of the electric feeder.

Their distance, according to my Leupold rangefinder, was nearly nine hundred yards; too far for my 7mm magnum and my long-range shooting ability to make an effective, clean one shot kill. There were no dirt roads down to the canyon's rim and too many gullies, so I could not drive closer. After a while, more doe and one small buck left the canyon by the same trails. Then I thought, "I've got my Realtree™ camouflaged, pop-up blind, that I can set up on the small hill overlooking the two trails that will get me close enough for a clear shot at 'El Viejo' if he's there and comes out." For that to work, I needed to quietly set up the blind this afternoon and leave it overnight.

I decided that was a good plan, so after waiting until noon and eating my lunch, I took my Sako out, loaded the magazine and put a round in the chamber, then shouldered it. Then I removed the lightweight pop-up blind and folding campstool from the bed of the pickup and began walking down the hill to the canyon's two trails. It occurred to me that I needed to be able to find the blind in the dark the next morning. I returned to my truck, removed the Garmin GPS from its dash mount, and put it in my parka pocket. While slowly walking, periodically I removed it and set waypoints along my path until I reached the slight hill.

Setting up the blind was easy with its lightweight pop-up poles held together by a rubber bungee cord running through the middle of each section. Unzipping the back and setting the folding camp chair inside, I placed large rocks on the four corners, where there were tie-down straps, just in case the wind began to blow in the middle of the night. "That should work." I thought. Then I quietly walked to my truck and made sure that I set a new waypoint where I was going to park the next morning.

After returning to the house, I had just pulled up to the back door when my cell phone rang and my friend, who owned the ranch, asked in a hoarse, raspy voice, "Stan, have you killed "El Viejo" yet." I laughingly answered, "No, Charlie. I have seen him but did not have a shot, so he is still out there. I think I know where he is bedding down though; in the shallow canyon ravine near the Double Mountain Buttes." Charlie said, "I think you're right because I've seen him go into that ravine by way of the two senderos leading into it. I always thought it would be easier to shoot him at the electric feeder near the food plot if I kept hunting long enough." I replied, "I think he's too wily and smart to feed where all the other deer are eating. That is why I have set up a pop-up blind overlooking the trails and senderos leading into the area. I'm going there tomorrow morning, long before sunrise and spend the day." I heard Charlie cover the telephone mouthpiece and start violently coughing and hacking in the background. Finally catching his breath, he said, "I'm sorry I can't be there to see you kill him, but this dadgum epizootic has me down, and I'm not going to be able to come there after all."

"That's okay Charlie. Stay in bed, eat chicken soup and drink plenty of liquids and an occasional Wild Turkey bourbon hot toddy. That will fix you up. "Adios, mi amigo y espero que tu mejores pronto, hombre." (Spanish: "Goodbye, my friend. I hope you get better soon, man." I said. Charlie replied, "Gracias, ten cuidado, Vato." (Spanish: "Thank you, be careful, dude.") Then he hung up.

I went into the house, changed clothes, built a fire and fixed supper. Afterward, I sat by the fireplace sipping my Dr. Pepper. Then, I thought, "I need to set my phone alarm for 4:00 a.m., that way I can be at the pop-up blind by 5:30 a.m. and let everything settle down by the legal shooting time of 6:30 a.m."

Early the next morning, after eating a light breakfast of cereal, I made a couple of ham sandwiches and put them, along with two fried pies in a ziplock bag and put everything in my backpack. I still had two bottles of water in it and made sure I had the most critical thing a hunter can carry out in the field; a roll of toilet paper! *(I have heard that prickly pear cactus pads are not a good substitute for it. Ouch!)*

I remotely started my truck and finished drinking my third cup of coffee. After making sure, the fireplace was banked, and the screen was safely in place; I walked out to the truck and drove in the direction of the canyon. The morning sky was crystal clear, and millions of stars were visible in the heavens. There was no wind blowing, and although the temperature was hovering around twenty degrees, I knew that my insulated clothing and boots would keep me warm in the pop-up blind. I followed the waypoints, on my Garmin GPS, until I reached the area at which I was to park the truck and then turned the engine off.

I removed the dash mounted GPS, put on my backpack, loaded my rifle, shouldered it and then began walking in the direction of the pop-up blind. I had my tiny Stream light flashlight with a red lens, which worked perfectly to illuminate the ground as I slowly, and quietly, followed the waypoints to the camouflaged blind. I arrived at it, opened the zippered back, stepped inside and sat down on the folding camp chair after removing my backpack and leaning the rifle in the corner. I took out my binoculars and put the strap around my neck, waiting for sunrise, which was still one hour away. Sitting there, I began to think about when my dad came home from Japan, at Christmas 1955, and all of us moved on January 1, 1956, to Williams Air Force Base in Mesa, Arizona, a suburb of Phoenix.

1956

ARIZONA GAMBEL'S QUAIL

IN MESA, ARIZONA, AT THE main gate of Williams Air Force Base, Dad showed his military ID to the white-helmeted air police guard. He saluted my father, who returned the salute, then gave him directions to base operations. Arriving at "base ops," Dad said, "I'll be here just a few minutes, and then we'll go to the base housing office and find out where we're going to live."

The day after Christmas, my dad, mother, sister Penny and I drove to Arizona in our new 1956 Buick Road Master two-door hardtop. All of the household goods, furniture and our clothes, except for what we had packed in bags in the car, was on a moving van and would arrive in about a week.

What an adventure; driving through the desert at night. I could barely contain my excitement as I lay on the broad shelf behind the back seat looking through the rear window glass at the full moon, the multitude of stars above in the black night sky and feeling the cold desert wind blowing through the partially rolled down windows. As we drove to Phoenix from the east, there were wide-open expanses of hard-packed desert terrain with many, fragrant smelling sagebrush plants, prickly pear cacti, and immense saguaro cacti looking eerily ghost-like in the moonlight. Early in the morning, dad stopped the car by the side of the road, and we watched a huge Gambel's quail covey run swiftly over the mostly barren ground. There were several hundred birds in the group, and they all ran in a closely coordinated, but helter-skelter formation, looking like gray flowing water; first going one direction and then instantly changing course and going another.

"Dad, those look like quail, are they?" I asked. "I think they are Gambel's quail with their top-notch on the head." He said. "Why are they running like that?" I asked. "That's probably a defensive maneuver that prevents predators, like coyotes and bobcats from catching them." My dad answered. "Are they good to eat?" I asked. "I suppose they're like any other quail and very tasty." He said. "Once we get settled in our new home, do you think will be able to go hunting for them?" I asked. "Probably, but we will have to find out when the hunting season opens." He replied.

When he came out of base operations, Dad got in the car and said, "Let's go to the base housing office now." Several of his friends who flew with him in Kimpo, Korea, and Kadena, Japan were assigned to Williams Air Force Base, and he had visited with them just a few minutes earlier. All of the officers, pilots and their families lived together in an area called "Wherry housing" which was approximately two blocks from the end of a new runway that was being built.

Dad came out of the base housing office carrying the set of keys to our new quarters. "Is everyone ready to see our new home?" He happily asked. We drove into the housing complex and found our one story, ranch-style, three-bedroom and one bath home with a single carport beside it. After opening the front door, we walked into the vacant house and looked around. Two small bedrooms were going to be my sisters and mine. Mother and Dad had a slightly larger one down the hall and across from the bathroom.

After walking around the house, my mother decided where each piece of our furniture was going to be placed and then we went into town and checked into a motel. We planned to stay there for a few days until the moving van arrived with our household goods. I had built several model airplane replicas of aircraft my father had flown in WWII and Korea and looked forward to hanging them from my bedroom ceiling suspended by fishing line.

A week later, the movers delivered everything to our new home, and we moved in. The air-conditioning system consisted of an evaporative swamp cooler which was mounted on the roof and provided cold, moist air to the bedrooms and house. That afternoon after pleading with him, my dad brought me some aeronautical sectional charts of the Phoenix and surrounding area.

Before my bunk beds, small writing desk and "chester drawers" were moved into my bedroom; I took the map charts, aligned one edge with another and, while standing on a folding step stool, attached them to a bedroom wall using staples. Taking two small "eye" screws, I placed one at the top center edge of the maps and another at the top far left. Threading the braided fishing line through them, I stuck a thumbtack through the knotted end of the line and placed it where Williams Air Base was located. Tying a sinker to the other end, and letting it hang several feet down to the floor, I was able to measure the straight-line distance anywhere in Arizona. Standing back and admiring my handiwork, I thought, "When I hang all of my model airplanes from the ceiling, my room will look like the flight planning room of base ops." I was happy with the way my bedroom looked.

A few days later, Dad came home from flying as an instructor pilot in T-28s and told me, "Quail season is open until the middle of February. In a few days, how would you like to go hunting with several friends of mine and me?" Jumping up and down and clapping my hands I said, "That will be so much fun!" Later that evening, I removed my Savage .22/.410 from its gun case, took out my gun cleaning kit and made sure the gun was clean and well oiled.

The following Saturday morning, Dad and I drove over to two of his friends' homes in the housing area and picked them up to go hunting. We headed east in the direction of the Superstition Mountains. One of dad's friends, Capt. Walt Binder was an avid bird hunter and knew where many of the quail coveys were located in the desert foothills. Driving down a dirt road on the hard-packed ground, we finally stopped after a large covey of Gambel's quail ran across the road.

Dad parked, and we all got out and loaded our guns. Everyone was shooting a Winchester Model 12 pump shotgun in twelve gauge except me. Looking down at me, Dad said, "Son, stay beside me the whole time and only shoot in front of you or up in the air and don't point your gun at the other hunters. Looking a little crestfallen, I said, "Dad I know all about hunter safety, and I would never point my gun at anyone." "Don't get upset; I just wanted to remind you that we all have to be safe, okay." He remarked and smiled. "Okay," I replied. We all lined up next to each other and started walking in the direction of the Gambel's quail that had crossed the road.

Quail hunters in Arizona spend the majority of their time pursuing three species of quail, Gambel's, Scaled and Mearns. Of these species, the Gambel's is by far the best known. Found throughout the state, this bird often is hunted in open desert country where they are more apt to run or flush than hold for a dog. The Gambel's jaunty, plumed topknot, carried by both sexes, makes for ready identification, along with the males bright russet cap, black face and bib and cream-colored belly marked with a black horseshoe. They are found throughout the Sonoran and Mohave deserts; through semi-desert grassland and in chaparral to the edges of pinyon-juniper woodlands and pine forests. [5]

After walking for a few minutes, we saw a large covey running in front of us. "Looks like we'll have to run them down, fellows!" Walt said. Then he took off running with the rest of us trailing behind. We caught up with the birds, and they scattered in all directions. As several ran close in front of me, I raised my .410 and fired at one, hitting it! "This is going to be easy." I thought.

Opening the action of my gun and replacing the spent shell with a new one, I picked up the bird and handed it to Dad who had also shot one and was putting it in the game pouch of his brown hunting jacket. Then he and I took off running after another nearby large covey we saw. The other hunters were going in different directions, so I no longer had to worry about shooting them or being shot. We spent the day running, shooting, reloading and picking up birds. The quail population in the area was vast and late in the afternoon we decided to stop hunting and return to the car.

Arriving there, Dad began to take the birds out of the game pouch of his jacket and lay them on the floorboard of the trunk. In all, he had killed twelve quail with his 12-gauge pump shotgun, and I had killed five with my single shot .410. "That's going to give us a nice mess of birds for dinner tonight." He said. In a few minutes, the two other hunters arrived with their game pouches full of quail.

After driving back to the base and dropping off Dad's friends, we pulled into the carport at our house. My mother and sister came out to greet us as Dad opened the car's trunk. "They are so beautiful and cute. How can you kill them?" My mother asked. Dad laughingly answered, "Point the gun and pull the trigger is all." My mother squinted her eyes in a mock scowl and shook her finger at him saying, "We'll have them for dinner tonight as soon as you clean them." Turning to me, Dad said, "Son, as the newest member of the hunter clan, you get to clean all the birds." "I'll be happy to clean all the birds if you will keep taking me hunting, okay?" I said. "We've got a deal; shake on it." He said while sticking out his hand. We shook on it, and from then on, I cleaned all the game we shot. It was worth it as far as I was concerned.

I enjoyed living in Arizona at Williams Air Force Base, but our stay only lasted one year until January 1957. Then we packed up everything and moved to Webb Air Force Base in Big Spring, Texas where my dad was assigned as a T-33 jet instructor pilot. We lived there for a little over two years until my parents divorced in 1960 and we moved to Levelland, Texas where we again lived with my grandparents.

Chapter Seven

CANYON SANCTUARY SURPRISE

AT SUNRISE, THE HIGH CIRRUS clouds began to take on a bright reddish, pink hue. "Red sky in morning, hunter take warning." I softly paraphrased the famous nautical quote, while admiring the beauty of the clouds. Then, on one of the senderos, I saw a large doe walking along followed by a yearling. A few minutes later, "El Viejo" stepped out from behind a large cedar bush and began walking up a different narrow trail leading out of the canyon. Reaching for my rifle, I laid the forend on my adjustable tripod shooting sticks next to the open window. Quickly turning the parallax knob until the sight picture was very clear; I set the variable scope on twelve power and estimated the distance to the big deer to be about three hundred yards. "Perfect. Now I've got you." I thought to myself as I watched him slowly move along the trail and walk behind a large group of cedars. Waiting for him to come out the other side; I "snicked" off the gun's safety and placed my index finger on the trigger. Seconds went by, then several minutes.

After waiting ten minutes, I put the gun's safety back on but continued looking through the rifle scope at the cedars. "Where'd he go?" I thought. Then I noticed slight movement below where he had disappeared into the cedars. Shifting my point of aim lower, I saw "El Viejo" emerge from behind the lower edge of the cedars and take off running. Quickly turning the safety off, I tried to follow the zigzagging deer as he ran deeper into the canyon, but there were too many cedars, poplar trees and other obstacles for me to get a clear shot. "What in the world scared him?" I thought, as I sat there puzzled and watched him run.

Suddenly coming into view, I saw a huge mountain lion running after the deer. "Holy crap! That is not something you see every day while hunting deer. If I can kill "El Viejo" and the mountain lion; what a magnificent taxidermy mount that will make." Then, in a flash, both disappeared into the dense underbrush and darkness of the canyon. "I didn't realize that mountain lions are this far north," I said aloud. "Wow. This is going to get interesting now."

I had never killed a "panther" before and had only seen a solid black one many years earlier when I had a deer lease in West Texas. Once, while working on the ranch, in the summer of 1961 at the age of sixteen, I was on horseback looking for stray cattle near the Concho River when I heard a loud growling, "scream" nearby and the quarter horse I was riding "spooked" and nearly threw me off. Finally reining in the gelding I was able to stop him. However, the horse's "wall-eyed" look told me we had just encountered something that he had a primordial and innate fear of and instinctively reacted by bolting away.

Mountain lions are large, slender cats with small heads and very long tails. Their fur is light, tawny brown color. As apex carnivores, they hunt and kill mostly white tail deer, mule deer, javelina pigs and feral hogs. Males are solitary animals weighing up to one-hundred-eighty pounds and are found in remote mountains, canyon lands, or hilly areas with good cover. The home range of an adult male may vary from eighty to two hundred square miles.

Standing up quickly, I unzipped the ground stand's back door and ran down the hill to the bottom of the canyon and the dense cedar brush and poplar trees.

"If I can intersect their path, I might get a shot at both of them." I thought to myself as I stopped next to a large tree, bending over at the waist and breathing heavily.

"El Viejo" suddenly burst out of a nearby, large stand of cedar bushes and nearly ran over me. Jumping aside, I raised my rifle and turned to fire at him. Then, I heard a "bloodcurdling" guttural, deep growl close behind me. The sound made the hairs on the back of my neck stand up. With my rifle at my shoulder, very slowly I turned around and saw the large snarling cougar ten feet away with his teeth bared. He was lying down on his haunches ready to pounce, his long tail nervously twitching from side to side and staring intently at me with his large yellow eyes. When I pointed the rifle at the big cat, I realized the scope was set on twelve power, and I could not see the crosshairs to take the shot because he was too close. Sliding the safety off with my right thumb, it made a soft "click." Instantly, the big cat lunged forward and brushed past my right leg in pursuit of the deer. Swinging around, I fired at the rear of the fleeing cougar and saw the bullet strike the ground to its right. "Well, crap." I thought, as I quickly worked the bolt, ejecting and loading another shell. Then everything was quiet, and both animals were gone. Standing there, I didn't know what to do next as my heart pounded rapidly in my chest.

After a while, I walked back to the pop-up stand. Sitting down, I knew there was no point in staying at the blind because "El Viejo" and the big cougar were long gone. Finally catching my breath, I gathered up everything, put my backpack on and walked to the truck.

Starting it, I thought, "Nobody will ever believe me when I tell them about this." What had just happened was a once in a lifetime set of circumstances that few hunters ever get to experience and I began to smile thinking about it. "Oigame, "El Viejo" y gato grande, manana esta un otro dia. Hasta la vista." (Spanish: "Listen to me, "Old Man" and big cat, tomorrow is another day. Until I see you then.") I murmured to myself.

Heading back to the house, I slowly drove by the food plot and automatic feeder and stopped on the road nearby. On the ground under it was a large covey of bobwhite quail intently feeding on the milo grain. "I'll hunt and quail this afternoon," I said aloud.

Sitting there, I replayed over in my mind what had just happened; remembering the goosebumps that popped up on my forearms and the hair standing up on my neck as the mountain lion throatily snarled close behind me. Then I smiled as I remembered the first time I ever got goosebumps many years before.

1957

RATTLESNAKE WRANGLER

CLIMBING A LIMESTONE ROCK OUTCROPPING, I reached up, put my right hand on an overhead rock ledge to look into a small cave entrance, and touched a rattlesnake sunning itself there. Instantly, I jerked my hand away. Raising my face up to see in the cave I was only two feet away from the rattlesnake as we stared intently at each other and goose bumps rose up on my arms, neck, and a chill ran down my spine. The big snake was furiously shaking its rattles and was tightly coiled in its striking posture; head raised, split tongue flicking rapidly and on full alert. Quickly, dropping my head down below the ledge and away from its strike zone, I thought "Oh man! That was close." The men in my family had warned me, "When climbing on a rocky outcropping, never put your hand anywhere before seeing if a snake or scorpion is laying there." Now, I understood their advice and the lesson was indelibly imprinted on my brain forever.

We were living in Big Spring, Texas and it was early summer. I had ridden my bicycle, carrying my Savage .22/.410 shotgun, about a mile away from my house to a large mesa on the south side of town. There were massive rockslides and limestone outcroppings on its slopes where I hoped to find, and kill some rattlesnakes. My family and I had spent the previous Easter at the ranch with my

Aunt Sally and Uncle Mac and my cousins. My dad and I were riding with Mac, to check on some cattle, when a huge rattlesnake crossed the dirt road in front of his pickup.

He stopped the truck, reached into the glove compartment; removed a .22 long rifle Smith & Wesson Model 18 Combat Masterpiece pistol from a fleece lined shearling holster; walked over to the snake and shot it in the head. After making sure it was dead, he picked it up by the tail and threw it in the back of the pickup saying, "Stan Jr., when we get home I'll skin it and show you how to tan the hide and make hatbands from it. There are several western wear stores in Big Spring that will buy them from you after they are cured, and they can be fitted onto a cowboy hat. That way you can have some extra spending money." "That would be great." I excitedly remarked.

As soon as we arrived at the house, Mac took the dead rattlesnake from the pickup bed, and we went down to the barn where he had a five-foot piece of one-half inch rebar stuck in the ground near one corner of the building. After taking out his pocketknife, he cut what was left of the snake's head off. Inserting the headless snake at the top of the rebar, he slid it down to the ground, saying. "Now it's going to be easy to slit the skin down its belly and peel the hide the off." After making the extended cut, he carefully began to pull the snakeskin away from the flesh and gently scraped it to remove any fleshy residue. Within a few minutes, it was loose except for the fifteen rattles, which he cut off. Then rolling the skin up, with the scales against each other, he walked into the adjacent barn shop and found a dusty quart-size Mason jar. Placing the moist skin in the jar, he went over to a shelf and removed a half-gallon can of isopropyl alcohol and a container of glycerin. Mixing equal parts of both, in a separate jar, he poured the solution into the one with the snakeskin.

Tightly screwing the lid on the jar, he gave it to me saying, "In three days, the hide will be cured, and you can remove it. Take it out and dry it, then hang it up in a darkened area for two days. At that point, it will be soft, pliable and you can take it to the western wear stores and see if they'll buy it from you." "How much should I ask for it?" I asked. He replied, "A big one like this should go for twenty dollars." I thought to myself, "Oh my gosh, that's a month of allowances for me. I think I can find more rattlesnakes in the rocks near my house and tan more snakeskins." I asked Mac, "Where can I get the glycerin and alcohol." He answered, "MacDonald's lumber and hardware store is a few blocks from your house, and they'll have it." Then my dad said, "Hold on a minute, Son. Are you going to start hunting rattlesnakes now? "Yes, sir, if that's okay," I answered. "I'm not sure it's such a good idea." He said. "Well, I killed two rattlesnakes and cut off their rattles two years ago when I was ten years old while hunting for prairie dogs, remember?" I said to him. "Yes, I remember, but I'll need to think about this for a while and talk to your mother too." He said. Feeling somewhat disappointed, I walked back to the house with Dad and Mac.

A few days later, after we arrived home, my dad came in from flying T-33's at Webb air base and said, "Your mother and I've decided it is okay for you to hunt rattlesnakes, just be sure they are dead before you handle them. Let's go down to the hardware store, and I'll buy your first batch of alcohol and glycerin. After that, you are on your own to buy supplies. Okay?" "Yes, Sir!" I said enthusiastically. So, after that talk, I became a "Rattlesnake Wrangler" and a young entrepreneur.

While hunched down, from my close encounter with the rattlesnake I had just touched, I opened the action on my Savage .22/.410 single shot making sure a shotgun shell was loaded. Then I quietly walked around to the top of the outcropping and could see the rattlesnake ten feet below me. Taking careful aim at the snake, I fired at its head with the number six shot pellets and hit it. It began to thrash around violently as I safely watched from above. Once it stopped moving, I slipped down to the ledge where it lay.

Slowly maneuvering to it, I heard several rattlesnakes loudly buzzing. Very carefully, looking into the dark cave opening, I saw two more rattlesnakes coiled and ready to strike. Opening the action of my gun, I slowly removed the spent shell and replaced it with a fresh one. Carefully raising the shotgun to my shoulder, I fired at the head of the closest snake killing it. Quickly reloading, I shot at the rattlesnake next to it, killing it too. Now I had three dead rattlesnakes to skin and cure. With the one Mac had given me that totaled four equaling eighty dollars if I could sell them all. I never had that much money before. After the snakes quit wiggling, I picked them up, hung them around my neck and climbed down the steep slope to my bicycle, where I set them in the front basket. I put the shotgun in its case, which was tied to the horizontal crosspiece of the bike.

Riding home, I was pleased with the way the day had gone and excited about skinning and curing the rattlesnake's hides and selling them. Had my Granddad been there, he would have told me, "Now, you're cooking with gas, for sure."

Once I arrived at the house, I went through the back gate and unloaded the snakes next to the fence. I had already driven a one-half inch piece of rebar behind the house where I could skin the rattlesnakes out of sight of my mother and little sister who were both very squeamish about my new venture.

After skinning, the snakes and curing the hides for several days, my dad took me to the largest western wear store in downtown Big Spring. While he waited in the car, I walked inside with a large paper sack containing the four tanned hides. An older man walked over and laughingly asked, "What can I do you for?" I answered, "I've got four tanned rattlesnake skins that I want to sell. Y'all can make hatbands out of them to put on cowboy hats." Opening the paper sack the man, who was the owner of the store, took them out and set them on the counter saying, "Son, where did you get these? Steal them off, somebody? "No, sir, I killed, skinned and tanned them myself," I told him. Oddly looking at me he said, "You don't say. How much do you want for them?" "I'll sell them for eighty dollars," I answered. He thought a moment then said, "I'll give you forty dollars cash for the lot." Not answering him or saying a word, I reached over the counter and began to put the snakeskins in the paper sack. "Now, hold on a minute, kid. What if I pay you fifty dollars?" He asked. "No, sir. I'll sell them to your competitor down the street for eighty dollars." I said, while somberly staring him in the eyes, not smiling or blinking. "Son, where did you learn to dicker like this?" He asked and then started chuckling.

Seeing that I was not smiling, he asked, "Okay, how many of these can you get?" "How many do you want?" I replied. "All you can make." He answered. "Then I'll bring you at least five each week, and I'll guarantee they'll be at least five feet long after they're tanned. But, I'll not sell them for less than twenty dollars apiece."

Pausing to think a moment, he said, "Okay, we've got a deal. Wait here a minute, and I'll bring you your money." Going to the cash register, he took out four twenty dollar bills and handed them to me. "What's your name?" Not smiling, I answered, "Stan Corvin, Jr. and I'll be back in two weeks from today with five more tanned rattlesnake skins." Then I turned and walked out the door as he stood there rubbing his hand over his sweaty baldhead, looking slightly amused and a little confused.

Opening the car door, I sat down in the passenger's seat and held up the four twenty dollar bills for my dad to see. "Son, I'm proud of you and amazed that you found something that pays that kind of money." He said while tousling my hair and beginning to drive in the direction of our house. "The man inside the store said he'll buy all of the rattlesnake skins I can tan, so I'll need more isopropyl alcohol and glycerin. Can we go to the hardware store so I can buy more?" I asked. "Okay." My dad said.

After I paid for the supplies and two more boxes of number six .410 shotgun shells, we went out to the car. I asked, "Can we stop by the Wagon Wheel Drive-In barbecue restaurant and get sandwiches and fries for supper? I'll pay for them."

Dad looked at me and said, "Sure, if that what you want to do. Stan Jr., you're the most unusual child I've ever known." I grinned at him saying, "I know I'm different than other kids, but don't forget I'm yours." He laughed as we drove to the drive-in restaurant.

For the rest of the summer and early fall, until they began to hibernate, I hunted, killed and tanned rattlesnakes making sure they were all over five feet long with their head and tails removed. After I sold my second batch, I bought a pair of Wellington rough out boots to protect me from snakebites since I had been wearing only sneakers while climbing the rocky slopes. Two weeks later, I bought a white straw cowboy hat with a rattlesnake headband.

In five months, I made two thousand three hundred dollars, which I deposited into my savings account at the bank. Later that year I learned that my mother, who taught fifth grade, made only two hundred forty dollars per month salary while I was making five hundred dollars selling rattlesnake skins. I was sad to think about how teachers were paid so little and how much time and dedication they put into the job. Frequently, in the evening I helped my mom grade papers so that she would not have to stay up late working. She was an excellent teacher, and all her kids loved her.

Chapter Eight

QUAIL HUNTING

ARRIVING AT THE HOUSE, I stepped out of my truck, removed my twelve gauge semi-automatic Beretta model 391 from the gun rack on the back window and laid it on the back seat. I had purchased the shotgun sixteen years earlier in Dallas and shipped it to Briley gunsmiths in Houston where I had it customized to my specifications. The twenty-eight-inch vent ribbed barrel was back bored to .733 diameter and the forcing cone extended to three and one-half inches. I also had the barrel ported to reduce the recoil, and the action polished to operate smoothly. I used it primarily to shoot in sporting clay tournaments and to hunt dove and quail.

Opening an ammo box containing a dozen boxes of my hand-reloaded shells, I took out a box of number seven and a half shot Winchester AA shotgun shells and put them in my insulated hunting coat laying on the back seat of the pickup. The weather had warmed up considerably but was still in the high thirties during the day, so it was chilly.

Walking into the house, I took a cold diet Dr. Pepper out of the refrigerator and put it, and two fried pies in a paper sack then went out to my truck. I drove back in the direction of the electric feeder and stopped at the mesquite tree with the reflective tape tied to a branch. Putting my bird hunting coat on, I loaded three shells in my shotgun and began to walk to the feeder.

I had not gone very far when I saw a bobwhite quail flush in front of me and fly away. Then, with the gun at ready, I slowly walked forward. A dozen quail burst from a nearby prickly pear cactus making a loud clattering noise as they flew. Quickly mounting the gun, I fired two fast shots and dropped two quail. Reloading, I put the two birds in the back game pocket of my jacket. When the covey had flushed, I saw several birds land about fifty yards away and began walking in that direction. As I passed the cactus, a single quail flew out, and I shot it. Reloading, I picked up the bird and put it away; then headed to where I had seen most of the covey land. As I walked along, several single birds flushed and I shot and killed each of them. Stopping to reload, I laughed as I remembered once reading Psalm 105:40 "He sent them quail and gave them manna." He had not given me any manna (although I did have two fried pies) but He sent me many quail, and soon I had ten in the game pouch of my hunting coat. I decided that was plenty for supper, so I went back to my truck; drank the soda and ate my fried pies.

Before returning to the house, I drove to the canyon and parked on top of the hill in hopes of seeing either "El Viejo" or the big cougar. However, after forty-five minutes of scanning the dense brush and senderos through binoculars and seeing no movement, I left and returned to the house.

Arriving there, I put the shotgun away, walked into the kitchen and unloaded all of the dead birds into the sink. After building a fire, I got a plastic garbage bag out and began to clean the quail. I suddenly stopped and smiled when I remembered cleaning quail with George Landreth in 1978. He was a renowned world-class big-game hunter and oilman from Midland, Texas.

It was November 1st and quail season was to start on the 15th. Earlier in the day, my uncle Jesse called me at my mortgage company office in Austin and asked if I would like to fly out to Midland and go hunting with him and several friends on opening day. He told me that a friend of his, George Landreth, had leased a pasture twenty miles north of town. "How many hunters will be hunting there?" I asked. "Sixteen," Jesse answered. "That's a lot of hunters for just one pasture," I said. There was a pause, and then he started laughing as he said. "The pasture is surrounded by a barb wire fence and contains eighty thousand acres; which is one hundred and twenty-five square miles. It's a small part of the Scharbauer ranch which has over five hundred thousand total acres." "Oh. Then I guess we don't have to worry about too many hunters." I said feeling somewhat embarrassed and chagrined for asking the question. "Why don't you fly in on the evening of the 14th and I'll pick you up at the general aviation terminal at the Midland Airport, and we will eat dinner at the country club," Jesse said. "That sounds great to me. I look forward to spending time with you and your friends and seeing the famous Scharbauer ranch." I replied.

After hanging up, I called a friend at the University of Texas, who was a professor of American history and offered to buy him dinner if he could quickly put together some information about the Scharbauer ranch. At dinner that evening, he gave me a folder containing an extensive dossier on one of the oldest and most famous ranches in the state of Texas.

In the 1880s, the ranch was established as a sheep growing operation, and then a cattle-raising enterprise covering nearly 500,000 acres (781 square miles) in West Texas and Southeast New Mexico. The ranch was home to seventy-five cowboys, five hundred saddle horses and tens of thousands of cattle and sheep. One of the ranches thoroughbred racehorses won the Kentucky Derby in 1979.

The vast ranchlands yielded significant oil production in the energy-rich Permian Basin region beginning in the 1940's. The Scharbauer family started the original First National Bank of Midland, donated land for the Midland Airport, established Midland Memorial Hospital, built and operated the large downtown Scarborough hotel. In short, they were a founding family and pillar of the community.

Earlier in June, I had purchased a six-passenger turbocharged Piper Cherokee T-tail Lance with a 300 horsepower Lycoming engine that cruised at two hundred miles per hour at twelve thousand feet altitude. Its range was almost eight hundred miles. The distance from Austin to Midland was three-hundred-seventeen miles, so the flight was approximately one and one-half hours from takeoff to landing.

After an uneventful flight on the 14th, I pulled up to the general aviation terminal at Midland Airport and saw Jesse sitting in a golf cart on the tarmac waving at me. Taxiing to a nearby parking area, I shut the engine down as he pulled up along the right side of my airplane. Unloading my hunting clothes and two shotguns, I tied the aircraft down and got in the golf cart next to Jesse. "Are you ready for some fast quail hunting." He asked. Looking a little perplexed, I remarked, "I guess so; what do you mean by fast quail hunting?" He laughed and said, "You're about to participate in a quail hunt orchestrated and controlled by George Landreth."

Driving to the Midland country club for dinner, I wondered, "What have I gotten myself into?" However, I trusted my uncle Jesse and knew that I was in for an exciting adventure. Early the next morning, we met George and the other quail hunters for breakfast at a downtown café. After eating, we all drove to the Scharbauer ranch "pasture" twenty miles north of town. Four of the hunters, including George, were driving Chevrolet Suburban's and towing trailers with familiar looking olive drab green painted army surplus jeeps strapped down on them. The "Jeeps," as they were called in US

Army parlance, were Model 151, one quarter ton MUTTS (Military Utility Tactical Trucks) and were similar to the ones I had frequently seen, and driven, while on my two tours in Vietnam as a helicopter pilot.

After driving through a cattle guard; we parked near the entrance to the pasture. The "Jeeps" were unloaded from the trailers and lined up next to each other. They had been immaculately restored to new military specifications (mil-specs) and were built on a metal unibody chassis with four-wheel independent suspension, having a seventy horsepower engine. With four speed transmissions, four-wheel-drive and CB radios with eight-foot whip antennas; they were excellent vehicles for hunting quail in the vast open pastures of West Texas.

When the military decided to replace them with the HUMVEE in 1978, all of the MUTTS were cut in half and destroyed because they were considered too dangerous for civilian use and for the general public to own. Their history of frequent rollovers was well known and documented. These four jeeps had been purchased and refurbished in Ciudad Juarez, Mexico and thus had never been never cut up.

"Okay everybody, gather round now and listen up." George barked out the order; eerily sounding like George C. Scott in the classic 1970 movie "Patton." Handing a sheet of paper to each of us he said, "I've assigned each of you to a MUTT. What we are going to do is form a line of them and begin to drive to the center of the pasture. I will be driving mine and be located next to the left outside vehicle. You can easily identify me by the OU (Oklahoma University) red pennant on my CB antenna." Pointing his finger at Jesse, he added, "You and Stan will ride with Bobby and me." The "Bobby" he referred to was Robert Braxton Holt, an icon in the ranching, banking and oil business in West Texas. Together they started the Midland Polo Club in 1964 and had been business partners, off and on, for thirty years.

Handing me a wooden hawk whistle, hanging from a leather lanyard, George said, "Stan put this around your neck and blow hard on it." I did as he asked and the whistle made the same shrill sound like a hawk. "Boys, each of the other jeeps has one whistle sitting on the front passenger seat and whoever sits there will use it. When we jump a covey of quail, I want the two outside jeeps to drive quickly on the other side of where the birds land and everyone gets out. Essentially, we will have the covey surrounded. I want the hunters with each of the whistles to start blowing them loudly as you approach the covey, that way the birds will not fly away. As they begin to flush, you can shoot straight up in the air or behind you, but not into the center. Everyone got that?" He said emphatically. We all nodded affirmatively. "All right then, saddle up and let's go." He said as he slid on the driver side of his MUTT.

I had never been on a hunt like this before and was amazed at George's organizational skills, which were executed with military-like command-and-control.

In 1970, he was selected as the recipient of the prestigious "Weatherby Hunting and Conservation Award." Given only to "hunters who have ethically taken the most varied, difficult and largest number of species in the world" the trophy was presented to him in New York City by Captain James A. Lovell, USN (Ret.); the famed NASA Apollo 11, 12, and 13 astronaut.

George had a large trophy room at his house where he kept the award in a glass case surrounded by full-bodied mounts of various big-game animals that he had killed, including a heavily tusked bull elephant in attack mode. Two massive mahogany doors guarded the entrance to the room. One of the doors had a tiny gold plaque attached to it at eye level saying, *"Enter reverently, this room cost me five million dollars. GHL."*

Driving fast across the dry, grassy, prairie pasture, I was amazed at how smooth the ride was with the MUTT's four-wheel independent suspension. We had not gone far when a large covey of bobwhite quail flushed and flew about a quarter of a mile away. The outer two jeeps sped up and drove on the opposite side of where the covey had landed. We stopped short of the birds, and everyone got out. "Stan start blowing the hawk whistle," George said as he began to walk slowly towards the quail. Everyone else had gotten out of their jeeps and formed a giant circle.

As the circle of hunters closed in on the quail, we began to see them run to a large stand of prickly pear cactus. Expecting them to fly, I readied my shotgun and continued to blow the whistle. Soon, all of the hunters were standing nearly shoulder-to-shoulder surrounding the cactus. I could see dozens of birds frantically running around in the middle of the prickly pear. One suddenly jumped up on a cactus pad in front of me and sat there nervously swiveling its head from side to side. After watching it for several minutes, I took the barrel of my shotgun and gently pushed it off the flat green cactus pad. "Whirr" was the loud sound of the covey as they all exploded out of the thorny sanctuary. Immediately, I raised and fired my over and under Winchester Model 101, 20 gauge straight overhead and hit two birds with consecutive shots.

Everyone else had shot and killed some birds too. Climbing back in the jeeps, we repeated the same hunting strategy all morning long. It was the most efficient way of hunting quail I had ever seen. At noon, we returned to the vehicles and trailers where a huge white tent with tables and chairs was set up. We ate a lunch that included barbeque brisket, potato salad, coleslaw, ranch-style pinto beans with ice-cold bottles of Heineken beer and chilled white wine. A restaurant in Midland catered it. I thought, "This is a lot more civilized than sitting on the ground eating cold Vienna sausages with saltine crackers and a purple onion."

We spent the rest of the afternoon using the same hunting method and jumped probably twenty more coveys of quail. At sunset, we returned to where we had started, and the jeeps were loaded on the trailers. "George, why don't you and Bobby come over to my house and we will fry up a bunch of birds for supper?" Jesse asked his two friends. "Sounds good to me." They each answered.

When we arrived at the house, we took two paper grocery bags full of dead birds into the kitchen and put them in the sink. "Stan, how fast can you clean a quail?" George asked me while smiling. "I'll bet you a case of Chivas Regal scotch that I'm faster than you." I cockily answered with a grin. George said, "Okay, let's each clean thirty birds and whoever finishes first, wins. Jesse, you're the judge." With that said, he began rapidly to clean the first bird. Suffice to say, within a few minutes, he had cleaned all thirty of his birds and I was still working on number fifteen. "There's a Pinkies liquor store about a block away. You can buy my case of whiskey now. I'll clean the rest of your birds and all the others too." Smiling sheepishly, I raised my hands and said "George, it's an honor to lose to you, sir. I'll be back in a few minutes." Then, I left and bought the case of whiskey.

We cooked all the quail and Jesse made mashed potatoes with gravy and a vegetable medley to go with them. It had been a fun and exciting day, and I now understood what Jesse meant when he asked me if I was ready for "some fast quail hunting." The next morning we went to the Midland Airport and then I flew back to Austin, Texas. It was a memorable experience, and I was impressed with Jesse's friends and the way George had orchestrated the hunt.

On February 10, 2014, George H. Landreth, age 86, was struck by an automobile and killed instantly while crossing the street on his way to the First National Bank of Midland, Texas. The 20-year-old driver of the car left the scene of the accident and was later arrested at his home.

After cleaning the quail, at the cabin, I rinsed them in the sink and dried them. I put a cup of flour in a bowl and rolled the quail in it until each breast was lightly coated. Then I poured some milk into another bowl and dipped each one in it before I again covered them with a thick layer of flour. I heated some lard in a big, cast iron skillet and then placed the quail breasts in it to fry while I made a salad and boiled some red new potatoes. When the quail breasts were golden brown, I put several on a plate along with the salad and potatoes, sat down at the kitchen table, and ate. Once I finished supper, I washed the dishes, put them in a drying rack by the sink, and sat down in the rocking chair by the fireplace with a Dr. Pepper. It had been a good day, and I was content to relax and ruminate about the quail hunting and my Scharbauer ranch adventure with my uncle Jesse and George Landreth.

Then I said aloud, "George if there are mountain peaks in heaven, you are probably sitting on top of one looking through binoculars for bighorn sheep which were your favorite game animal to hunt." Rest in peace, amigo.

1958

SPRINGFIELD 30-06

IT WAS EARLY JUNE, AND I was lying on my stomach in my lower bunk bed reading the latest issue of American Rifleman Magazine published by the National Rifle Association (NRA). A year earlier, I had joined the organization by using some of the money from my rattlesnake skin enterprise and received the magazine monthly. Near the back of the publication, I saw an NRA advertisement for the sale of surplus US Army 1903-A3 Springfield bolt action rifles in 30-06 caliber. The price was $29.95 plus $3 for shipping. Sitting up, I excitedly thought, "I can afford that." The advertisement said the rifles were manufactured in 1944 and packed in cosmoline grease and had never been fired. The "A3" designation meant the gun barrels had four lands and grooves which greatly enhanced their accuracy. There was an address at the bottom of the ad from which the rifle could be ordered if the buyer was at least twenty-one years old. I thought about the requirement for a moment and saw there was no request for age verification, only a certification the buyer was twenty-one.

Thinking, "I would rather ask for forgiveness than permission," I went into the kitchen where my mother was fixing supper and asked if I could borrow her portable typewriter and have some blank paper and an envelope. She said, "That's okay. Just be careful because I use the typewriter while teaching school." I assured her that I would. Setting up the typewriter on my desk, I wrote a letter requesting that a Springfield 30-06 rifle be mailed to me and enclosed was a postal money order for $32.95.

I also stated that I was twenty-one-years-old. (I had turned thirteen in May.) Signing the letter with a flourish, so that it did not look like a child had written it; I folded the paper and placed it in the envelope. Opening my desk drawer, I took out my moneybox and removed two twenty dollar bills. Taking the typewriter back to my mother's closet, and then walking out the front door, I yelled, "I'm going down to Edward's house, but will be back in time for supper." Edward was my best friend and lived about a block away. I got on my bicycle and rode to the post office substation a mile away from my house. Going inside, I told the clerk I needed a money order for $32.95 made out to the NRA. After paying for it, and a four-cent postage stamp, he gave me my change. I put the money order in the envelope, placed a stamp on it and dropped it in the mail slot. Riding my bicycle away from the post office, I could barely contain my excitement.

Returning home, I yelled to my mom that I was back and she answered saying, "Dinner will be ready in about thirty minutes." In my bedroom, I looked through a large stack of old American Rifleman Magazines, that my uncle Mac had given me, and found an article reviewing and discussing the Springfield model 1903-A3. I read and studied the article that described the rifle specifications and ballistics and how to disassemble and assemble it for routine cleaning and maintenance.

"Dinner is ready," my mother yelled down the hall to my sister and me. On the way to the dining room, I decided not to say anything about buying the rifle. Only the three of us were having supper because four months earlier my dad had been sent to Edwards

Air Force Base in California on a temporary duty assignment (TDY) as one of three test pilots flying the newly built T-38 Talon twin-engine jet trainer. He was scheduled to return in September when the flight-testing was completed for the new airplane.

Sitting at the table, I was quietly lost in thought about my new rifle when my mother announced, "In three days I will start teaching remedial reading for the summer session of school. Stan, Jr. you will have to look after your sister Penny each day while I am gone. The classes end at 1:00 p.m. so I will not be gone very long." Groaning, I said, "How am I supposed to go kill rattlesnakes with Penny in tow?" My mother frowned at me and said, "Under no circumstances are you to take her hunting with you. You will have to wait until I come home before you leave. Do you understand me?" Reluctantly, I said, "Yes ma'am." Sullenly picking at my food, I finished dinner and asked: "May I be excused now?" My mother said, "Okay" so I picked up my plate, silverware, and glass and rinsed it out it in the kitchen sink.

Back in my room, I got my gun cleaning kit out and looked through the contents of it. I realized that I did not have a thirty caliber-cleaning rod and would need to get one before the new rifle arrived. I thought, "Tomorrow I'll ride my bicycle down to McDonald's hardware store. I'll bet they have them."

After breakfast the next morning, I rode my bike to the store and looked through their assortment of gun accessories. I found the cleaning rod I needed and started walking to the cashier to purchase it when I noticed several shelves with various calibers of ammunition boxes stacked on them. Finding the boxes of 30-06 ammo, I realized I didn't know what bullet weight to use in my new gun. I planned to hunt deer with it at the ranch when we went there for Christmas.

I asked a nearby clerk, "What is the best 30-06 ammo to shoot whitetail deer?" Coming over to the shelf, he handed me a box of

Winchester 150-grain Silver Tip bullets, saying, "Most deer hunters use these." They cost five dollars, and with the change, the postal clerk gave me the day before, I had just enough money to buy the cleaning rod and the ammunition. After I paid for everything and set the items in my handlebar basket, I rode home and put them away in my closet.

In a few days, my mother started teaching school, and I anxiously waited for the mail carrier to appear each morning. After two weeks, he walked up to our front porch carrying a long cardboard box and a handful of mail. I had been sitting on the front porch each day waiting for him. Taking the box and mail inside, I left the envelopes on the kitchen table and took the box with my new gun back to my bedroom. As usual, Penny was in her bedroom with her door closed listening to loud Elvis Presley 45 RPM phonograph records.

After cutting open the box with my pocketknife, I lifted the rifle out and unpacked it from the brown, heavy waxed paper. The gun was completely coated in thick cosmoline grease. Setting it on a newspaper on my glass topped desk, I went out to the garage and found some paint thinner and rags which I used to remove the heavy grease. After an hour, the rifle was clean, but I had a severe headache and was very dizzy. I heard Penny's door burst open and she ran into my bedroom. "What is that smell?" she yelled at me. I said, "It's cleaning solvent. Get out of here!" She grumbled something then slammed my bedroom door shut as she went out. I realized I had not opened any windows for ventilation and that was why I was feeling bad.

I opened all three of my windows and let the room air out. Afraid that Penny was going to say something to my mom, I went to her bedroom door and asked, "How would like to go to the 7-11 with me and get an ice cream cone?" She slowly opened her door looking somewhat shocked and said, "Really. You're not just kidding?" I said, "No, you can ride my bike with me to get them."

We went to the store, I bought two ice cream cones, and we ate them as we walked back to the house. When we arrived there, Penny ran to her room, yelled, "Thanks" and slammed her door. My room had a faint odor of paint thinner, but it was not too bad, and I knew my mother would not come into it when she got home from school because she knew that I kept the jars of rattlesnake skins under my bed and she was afraid of them.

For the next hour, until my mother came home, I carefully inspected all of the components of my new rifle. Removing the bolt, and looking at its face, I saw there were no marks, indicating the gun had never been fired. I took five 30-06 cartridges and loaded them into the magazine. Then I realized the only way to unload them was to cycle them into the chamber individually. Being careful not to touch the trigger, I removed all of the cartridges. Thinking, "There's got to be a better way of removing unfired shells." I got out my well-worn and dog-eared Stoegers gun catalog and after looking through it; I found a replacement magazine box with a hinged floor plate and trigger guard combination. It was only a twenty dollars, so I decided to order one in a few days and replace the existing one.

Included in the box with the rifle was a brown leather military style shoulder strap. I installed it through the sling swivels on the fore end and rifle butt. Loosening it, I slung the gun over my back and marched around my small bedroom thinking, "Maybe someday, I'll be a soldier when I grow up." Little did I realize that ten years later I would be in war-ravaged South Vietnam, flying helicopters for the US Army.

Several nights later, I was awakened by my mother shaking my shoulder and whispering "Wake up, I think somebody is trying to steal the hubcaps off our car! Load your gun and come with me."

Jumping up I put my bathrobe on and loaded my Springfield's magazine and chambered a round.

We walked to the front door where my mother quietly opened it. She and I walked down the steps and around the corner of the house where we saw two teenage boys removing the left front and rear hubcaps. She yelled loudly, "Get out of here right now, we've got a gun!" I raised the rifle to my shoulder and turned the safety off while pointing it at the boys. Immediately they jumped up, dropped the hubcaps and began to run swiftly down the street. Looking through the rear peep sight, I placed the front post on the back of the last boy and thought, "Hmm, it would be a lot easier to shoot him than a small prairie dog." My mother urgently said, "Stan, Jr. do not shoot!" As she quickly placed her hand on the barrel and forced me to lower it. "Aw, Mom I wasn't going to shoot him." She stood there and looked at me strangely and curiously. That was the first time I understood a gun was the "great equalizer."

After picking up the two hubcaps, we went inside, and she called the police, but they did not come out because the teenagers had already run away leaving the hubcaps behind. I unloaded my rifle; put it in the closet and went to bed, but had trouble going to sleep because my adrenaline was surging and my heart was beating hard. After a while, my mother came in my room and sat on the side of my bunk saying, "I'm proud of you. You are a lot more mature than most boys your age. Did you unload and put your .22 away?" "Yes, ma'am," I said, realizing that she did not know that I had loaded my Springfield rifle and had it with me during the confrontation. Kissing me on the forehead, she stood up and said, "Get some sleep now."

In September, my dad returned from Edwards Air Force Base in California, and after a few days, I decided to tell them about my new rifle. One afternoon, after coming home from Webb Air Force

Base, he was in an unusually good mood because he learned that he was on the promotion list for major. Sitting down next to him on the sofa I asked, "Dad, can I show you something in my room?" He looked at me and said, "Is this about your rattlesnake skins?" I answered, "No, sir." Looking a little amused, he got up, and we went to my bedroom where I opened my closet and took out the Springfield 30-06 and handed it to him. "Where did you get this?" He asked. "I ordered it from the NRA magazine, and they mailed to me a few months ago," I replied. "It doesn't look like it's ever been shot." as he raised the stock to his shoulder and looked through the sights. "The ad says they've never been used," I remarked. "I paid for it with my own money. Is it okay if I keep it?" I asked. Lowering the rifle he asked, "You lied about your age to get it, didn't you?" Nodding my head, I answered, "Yes sir, I did, but there was no age verification requirement, so it was a small fib."

Laughing, my dad said, "Although you are only thirteen-years-old you act more like you are twenty-one. Your mother told me about you running off the hubcaps thieves. Was this the gun you had loaded?" I answered, "Yes, sir. But I would not have shot them unless they tried to hurt Mom or me." "Son, I do believe you were born one-hundred years too late. You would have made a great young pioneer, and yes, you can keep the gun. Just don't say anything to your mother about it." He handed the rifle back to me and walked out of the bedroom.

In a few weeks, Dad took me to a gun show at the local convention center, and I bought one hundred rounds of 30-06 armor piercing ammo for four dollars. Afterward, we went to a gravel pit south of town and shot the rifle. With a steel butt plate, it had a lot more recoil than my .410, but I was determined not to let that bother me, although a few days later I had a sizable bruise on my right shoulder.

Four years later, in 1962, I spent a year converting the Springfield into a sporting rifle with a fancy walnut stock, deeply blued action, shortened barrel and a Redfield 3x9 Widefield telescope on it. I still have the gun today, although it does not look at all like the rifle I bought from the NRA.

Chapter Nine

CRITTER DECOY

AT 5:00 A.M., THE ALARM clock going off on the nightstand next to the bed abruptly awakened me. Turning over, I pressed the snooze button. I had been dreaming about flying helicopters in South Vietnam on my first tour in the combat zone in 1968. I rarely thought about the war anymore; however, I suppose with my isolation at the hunting cabin and the chilling encounter with the cougar a few days earlier; long-buried feelings of a time I spent "hunting" enemy soldiers were triggered. For the most part, I was asymptomatic for post-traumatic stress disorder (PTSD); however, sudden loud noises startled me and the sound of a helicopter flying nearby always caused my heart to beat faster.

Yawning and stretching, I sat on the edge of the bed and quickly forgot about my dreams. I dressed and went into the kitchen and put on a pot of coffee, then added some kindling and logs to the still smoldering fireplace. I heated the oven to 350°, opened a can of biscuits, and put them in the oven. Then I pan-fried several thick slices of venison sausage, which I had brought with me. After my meal of fried quail the night before, I was not very hungry but knew that I needed to eat later on to counteract the time-release heart and diabetes medication I took daily.

Sitting by the fireplace and drinking my cup of coffee, I thought about the way I would approach my hunt for "El Viejo" today. "I'm pretty sure that he stays in the area where my ground stand is set up next to the sendero, so I will spend the morning walking in the nearby ravines and canyons and see if I can get a shot at him."

In the rocky terrain, walking up on a deer was almost impossible because of the "crunching" noise my boots would make as I walked on the gravel. Mule deer, named for their large ears, have excellent hearing and the slightest sound will alert them to nearby danger or the presence of another deer. I needed a distraction to keep "El Viejo" from hearing me. A few weeks earlier, I had been hunting varmints and using my electronic game call with a remote-controlled furry "critter" decoy, which flopped around on the ground to attract coyotes and bobcats. I went outside to my pickup, started it, and then brought the equipment in and set it on the kitchen table. I checked to see if the NiCad battery was still fully charged for the decoy and saw that it was. "If I set this near to the ground stand and turn in on, it should last for several hours on the low setting before the battery dies. That may distract the deer from any sound he may hear as I'm walking in the ravine." I laughed at the thought of using a varmint decoy to hunt a large mule deer.

Finishing my coffee and banking the fire, I gathered all of my equipment, walked outside and loaded everything in the truck. The wind was blowing hard, so that also was going to help keep the deer from hearing me. In my pockets, I had four biscuits with sausage to eat later that morning. I drove to the ground stand and turned off the truck engine. It was still dark, so I quietly opened the door and carried the varmint decoy to an area about fifty yards downhill from the stand. Placing it on the ground next to a small cactus, I turned the power on with its remote control, and the furry "critter" began flopping around in the cactus pads while making a rustling noise. "This may just work." I thought.

Walking back to the truck, I waited for the sun to come up so that I could begin my "walkabout" as the Australian aborigines boys did for their rite of passage into manhood. I was well past my boyhood, and the Vietnam War had long ago turned me into a man. Especially after April 29, 1972, when I was shot down twice in ten minutes in my helicopter, and a rescue ship. Then I was hit five times in the chest, stomach and right leg with AK-47 bullets while trying to save a fighter pilot who had already been shot down at the DMZ.

Sitting there, and dozing slightly, I recalled a shooting competition at the Midland, Texas country club when I was fourteen years old. It was the first time I entered a tournament against grown men who were not members of my family and who badly wanted to beat a "dumb" kid who was competing against them.

1959

LIVE PIGEON SHOOT

"HELLO?" I SAID, AFTER ANSWERING the black rotary dial telephone sitting on a small table in the hallway of my home in Big Spring, Texas. "Stan Jr., this is Jesse. What have you been up to lately? Have you been shooting clay targets recently?" He asked. "Yes, sir. I've been doing my schoolwork during the week, hunting rattlesnakes and shooting skeet and trap nearly every weekend when I can get a ride out to the gun range at Webb Air Force Base." I answered. Jesse was my mother's brother and a geologist and petroleum engineer in the oil business in Midland, Texas. "Good!" He replied. "How would you like to come over here this Friday and shoot in a live pigeon tournament Saturday?" I asked, "What's a live pigeon tournament?" He laughed and said, "It's similar to shooting trap, but a man instead of a machine throws live pigeons. The bird has to be hit and fall inside a large, marked circle or it's considered a miss. Two misses and you are out of the competition and tournament. I've talked to your mom, dad, and Granddad and we think you will do well in the competition because you've been shooting and killing lots of dove ever since you were eight years old." Without hesitating, I said, "Yes. I would like to do it."

Jesse replied, "Good, I'll arrange everything, and you and your dad can stay with me at my home. Granddad is coming down from

Levelland to watch you shoot in the tournament. He will be staying here too. I will see you this Friday, but before you come here, try to shoot some trap from the twenty-seven-yard handicap position. That will be good practice for what you're going to be shooting in the live pigeon tournament."

After hanging up the telephone, I excitedly went into my room and took my Winchester Model 12 pump shotgun out of its case. Opening the action and checking to make sure it was unloaded; I disassembled the gun and ran a cotton oil patch down the barrel and oiled the bolt and trigger assembly. My parents had given me the shotgun two years earlier for a Christmas present. I used it primarily for hunting quail, dove and shooting skeet and trap clay birds.

A few months after getting it, I took it to a local gunsmith and using the money I earned from my rattlesnake skin enterprise, had him silver solder a three-eighths inch wide solid rib to the twenty-eight inch modified choked barrel. He also added a gold front bead and a small white mid-bead to the rib. When I first got the gun, I took four hundred grit emery cloth and jewelers rouge and spent several hours polishing the interior moving parts of the gun until they were mirror smooth. When lightly oiled, I operated it as fast as the semi-automatic shotguns J.C. Higgins, Remington, Winchester, Ithaca and other shotgun manufacturers, produced. Reassembling the gun, I put it away and checked to see how much ammo I had to shoot at trap targets the next day.

That evening at supper, I told my parents about the call from Jesse. My dad agreed to pick me up from my junior high school for the next two days and take me to Webb Air Force Base's shooting range where I could practice shooting at trap targets from the twenty-seven-yard handicap line. My mother and younger sister Penny decided not to go to the competition because they were concerned about killing "helpless" birds although they both liked to eat quail and dove.

Early Friday morning I packed a small bag, took all of my hunting equipment and shotgun, and put it in the trunk of my dad's car. After school on Friday, he picked me up, and we drove forty miles to Midland, where we met my uncle Jesse and Granddad at the country club for dinner. Sitting in the formal dining room at a cloth-covered table, Jesse asked, "Stan, Jr., how many clay trap targets did you hit from the twenty-seven-yard handicap line at the base shooting range yesterday?" "All fifty of them," I answered happily. Smiling at me and tousling my short burr cut hair, he said, "Atta boy. That's what I hoped you would say." Standing up, he "winked" at my dad and granddad and said, "I've got to go see a man about a dog. I'll be back in a few minutes." Looking surprised, I asked, "Is he buying a bird-dog?" My dad laughed and said, "No, he's probably going to talk to someone about the pigeon shoot tomorrow." A few days later, after the tournament, I learned that he had "bought" me in a Calcutta auction and paid a $1,000 entry fee for my participation in the shoot which was a lot of money in 1959.

The next morning I put my shotgun, gun cleaning kit and cloth-hunting vest in the back of Jesse's car. After drinking coffee and eating breakfast, we went to the country club located a short distance outside of town. Driving north past the main clubhouse and the golf course, we parked with a large group of automobiles and pickups near a cattle guard and walked over to several large white tents that had been set up in a flat, open pasture. Jesse filled out some paperwork and came back with a folded piece of white cloth with a number on it. Walking over to me, he turned me around and then took four small safety pins and attached the cloth to the back of my tan hunting vest. He said, "Now you are officially registered, and the competition will start soon. Let's go over to the field, and I'll explain how it works."

Walking a short distance to the shooting ring, Jesse said, "Stan, Jr., this is called live-bird Columbaire pigeon shooting. The bird is hand thrown up in the air in the direction of the circular ring in front of you by a Mexican man, called a Columbaire. The ring is approximately ninety yards in diameter, and you can see that a low fence about eighteen inches high has been set up to define its outer edges. Once the pigeon is thrown up in the air, you have to shoot and drop the bird within the boundary ring, or it is considered a "miss." You also must fire two shots at it, even if you hit it with the first one. That is the rule. The competition consists of thirty birds, which you will shoot in six rounds of five birds each. You will stand twenty yards behind the Mexican man who is sitting on a stool inside the ring with a cage of live pigeons beside him.

He is wearing a high-collared vest made of heavy saddle leather to protect him from being shot in the back with birdshot. I bought some "high brass" number seven-and-one-half shotgun shells for you to shoot. By plucking select feathers and throwing the pigeon high up and out into the ring in front of him, the Columbaire is going to try to make you miss the shot as the bird veers to the left or right because of the missing feathers. You will not be able to see what he is doing because the bird is on his lap and you are standing behind his back. So, I want you to stay focused, alert and say, "Pull" when you are ready for him to throw the bird. Remember it must land inside the boundary, and you have to fire two shots for each bird thrown. If you miss more than two birds, then you are automatically eliminated from the competition. Okay?" Grinning, I said, "Yes, sir. It sounds like it will be easier than hitting high-flying dove over the sunflower field at the ranch." Jesse smiled and said, "Nephew, I like your optimism. Good luck." Then he slapped me on the back and walked away.

In a few minutes, about forty shooters, including me, were led over to some temporary bleachers where we sat down and waited our turn to shoot. I was the only "kid" shooting, and most of the men were much older than me. Several had white hair like my grandfather. Many of them were carrying American made sixteen gauge L.C. Smith double-barreled side by side shotguns or beautifully stocked, over and under twelve gauge German made Merkel's, manufactured before World War II.

None of the shooters were using a "lowly" Winchester Model 12 pump shotgun. Sitting there, I heard several people behind me whisper, "Who's the kid?" Turning around, I smiled and confidently said, "I am Jesse Heath's nephew, and I doubt that you gentlemen can out shoot me." No one said anything more after my comment, but I could feel their hostility and smiled to myself. At the Webb Air Force Base's skeet and trap range, I frequently shot against older men who were expert marksman, and consistently beat them, so I was confident this contest would be no different.

Soon the first group of five shooters stood up and went over to the ring, and one man stepped inside and walked to an area marked by a three-foot square box. Raising his shotgun to his shoulder, the shooter called "Pull" and the Mexican threw a bird high into the air. After firing two quick shots, there was a large "puff" of feathers, and the bird fell into the ring. Reloading and yelling, "Pull" the second bird was thrown up in the air, but wobbling erratically, it rapidly flew off to one side. The shooter fired two shots and missed! Quickly reloading and standing still for a moment to compose himself, he called "Pull" for the third bird, and the Mexican threw it very high up in the air. The shooter fired both shells and missed with both shots. The pigeon landed well outside of the ring, without flying at all, because its neck had been broken before it was thrown. Unloading his over and under shotgun, he put it over his right shoulder and muttered "Well that's all for me today," and disgustedly stomped off the field kicking several dried cow patties as he went.

The remaining four competitors took their turns, and two hit all five pigeons. Three missed several birds and were immediately eliminated from the competition. Then my group of five shooters was called up. After the first shooter hit all five birds, it was my turn. I walked over to the square box, loaded two shells, raised the shotgun to my shoulder, placed my left foot in front, leaned slightly forward and called, "Pull." The Columbaire threw the first pigeon, and I hit it immediately after it left his right hand; then quickly fired the second shot and hit it again as it was falling to the ground. Slowly swiveling around on the stool, the Mexican squinted at me from under his large, straw, flat-brimmed cowboy hat and quietly said, as he held up his right hand, "Ten cuidado, joven. Tira mas despacio, por favor. Necesito mi mano derecho." (Spanish: Be careful, young man. Shoot more slowly, please. I need my right hand.")

I grimaced and replied, "Si, senor. Lo siento mucho. No volvera a suceder." (Spanish: "Yes, sir. I am very sorry. It won't happen again.") "Tu hables Espanol? ("You speak Spanish?) He asked. "Si, un poquito." ("Yes, a little bit.") I answered. "Muy Bueno, mi amigo. Muy Bueno." He replied. Then he toothlessly smiled at me, and I instantly knew that I had made a friend who might help me win the tournament. When he turned around, I noticed that his right arm and bicep was twice as large as his left; meaning he had been throwing birds for many, many decades.

He threw the remaining pigeons for me, and I hit all four. Walking back to the bleachers I sat down and thought, "This is a lot easier than shooting 27-yard clay targets or fast highflying dove."

The rest of the shooters took their next turns, and I did too. As the morning continued and we shot, I eventually hit all thirty pigeons. The other shooters, one by one, were eliminated from competition when they either missed more than two birds or failed to fire their second shot, which counted as a miss. Finally, only one tall, lanky, weathered-face cowboy remained in the competition with me. Sporting a white handlebar mustache covering all of his mouth, he was dressed in scuffed, black high-topped boots with the jeans tucked in and a heavily starched white western shirt. Wearing a classic light gray Stetson pushed back upon his "fish-belly" pale white forehead, he was smoking a hand-rolled cigarette. I saw he had a small cloth bag of "Genuine Bull Durham" cigarette tobacco in his shirt pocket with its drawstring tag hanging out. Each summer many of the Mexican cowboys, with whom I worked on my family's ranch in Sterling City, smoked the same brand of tobacco.

The cowboy had hit all thirty of his pigeons and fired all the required shots. We were called into the ring by the judges and told to shoot in rotation at five consecutively thrown birds until one of us missed a bird. That would determine the winner. After shooting first and hitting my five birds, it was his turn. He fired at the first pigeon thrown and hit it; then there was an audible sounding "click" when he pulled the trigger for the second shot. Opening the well-worn blued box lock action of his A.H. Fox side-by-side shotgun, he groaned and softly cursed when he realized the second shotgun shell had a defective primer and failed to fire; therefore, his second "shot" was scored a "miss."

Turning around and walking over to me, he said in a deep, gravelly voice, "Well son; it looks like you're the winner. Congratulations!" Then he stuck out his big calloused right hand. I shook it, looking a little dazed and confused. For a moment, I did not fully comprehend that the shotgun's failure to fire the second shell was the same as him missing the bird and was a costly mistake. My dad, grandfather, and uncle came running out to the ring and started pounding me on the back yelling, "You won! You won!" while again explaining the archaic rule about firing the second chamber. In the late 1800's all live pigeon shooting was done with double-barreled muzzleloading shotguns. If the bird was hit with the first barrel, then the second one had to be fired to render the gun safe.

When the festivities in the tents were over, I was presented with a small trophy and Jesse met with several of the pigeon shoot organizers, and they handed him a large manila envelope full of one-hundred dollar bills. In the car, Jesse handed me five-hundred dollars as my prize-winnings. Later at his home, he and my dad and grandfather split the remaining twenty-eight-thousand dollars first prize money from the seventy percent payout of the Calcutta. It had been a good day, and I was pleased to have won. Leaving Jesse's house early that evening, my dad and I drove back to Big Spring.

We picked up barbecue sandwiches at the Wagon Wheel Restaurant before going home and having supper with my mother and Penny, where I excitedly told them about the tournament and showed them my trophy. Many years later, Jesse told me the money he made from the Calcutta was his initial "grubstake" in the oil business where he later became extraordinarily wealthy and a multimillionaire.

CHAPTER TEN

WALKABOUT

ONCE IT WAS LIGHT ENOUGH to see the surrounding hills, I opened the door of my pickup, put on my coat and slung my rifle over my right shoulder after chambering a round. First looking at my Garmin GPS to set a waypoint for the truck's location and making sure the batteries were fully charged, I began my hike hoping finally to get a shot at "El Viejo." Quietly closing the door, I slowly walked down a game trail into the nearby ravine. Aware that I was near the area where I had recently encountered the big cougar, I was on high alert for any unexpected sighting of him and had already adjusted my riflescope to its lowest power setting so that I did not repeat my misadventure at our initial meeting.

Carefully watching the placement of each step, I silently descended the gravel trail to the bottom of the shallow canyon and the dry sandy creek bed there. Hearing faint rustling, I stopped and saw a nine-banded armadillo ahead of me scratching around some uprooted cedar stumps looking for grubs, insects, and worms. Although extremely nearsighted, their hearing is excellent with large pointed ears mounted on the top of their head. Not wanting it to run off, making noise, I waited for it to move away. Sensing danger, suddenly it stood up on its hind legs, braced itself with its tail and looked in my direction while sniffing the air for any scent. I remained motionless and made no noise. Soon, the creature resumed feeding and slowly wandered away.

The creek bed, lined on both sides with large poplar, cedar and mesquite trees, was still dark in the ravine. Sitting down and leaning back against one of the trees, I decided to wait until there was more light for me to see the surrounding terrain. Stretching out my legs I laid my rifle across them, leaned my head back on the tree trunk, and thought, "This hunt for "El Viejo" has become my version of a walkabout." As I recalled the ancient ritualistic spiritual and physical journey of the Aborigines, several of whom I met on an R&R trip to Australia in 1971 when I went there once while serving as in the US Army in Vietnam. I was staying in the "outback" at Alice Springs and traveled on a tour bus to Ayers rock, which they called "Uluru."

A walkabout is the aboriginal Australian hike that serves as a rite of passage for young boys entering into manhood and transforms them into adults. The trek takes place between the ages of ten and sixteen. Lasting up to six months, it requires the individual to live and survive alone in the wilderness wearing only a loincloth and going barefoot.

During a walkabout, the young person will sometimes travel a distance of over one-thousand miles. The participant must be able to make their own shelter and be capable of finding food and water for themselves to survive this long hike. That means he needs to hunt and kill game animals, catch fish, and also recognize and utilize edible and healing plants.

They must ultimately prove to the elders that they are capable of surviving the harsh environment of their native land. The walkabout also provides a time for self-evaluation, personal reflection and is both a journey across the desert and the mind.

After sitting by the tree for thirty minutes, I could see and stood up stretching before beginning silently to walk in the sandy creek bed. Carefully moving along, in a few minutes I faintly heard some "grunts" and squeals a short distance in front of me. Thinking, "Those must be feral hogs because I don't think javelinas are this far north in Texas." I quickly moved to one side of the creek bed where I stood next to a tree and waited.

Soon, several large feral sows followed by a dozen small piglets walked out from the shadows and into the dry creek bed. Then they turned and began slowly walking away from me, occasionally stopping to root around in small patches of ryegrass that were growing on the creek banks. I decided to wait until they were far away before I continued. "Don't just do something; stand there." I laughingly thought to myself as I paraphrased a long-held mantra I had adopted many years earlier.

A feral hog is a domestic pig that has escaped or been released in the wild and is living like a wild animal or is one that is descended from such animals. Approximately two-point-five million feral hogs live in Texas and cause about four-hundred million dollars in agriculture damage each year. Sows begin breeding at six to eight months of age and have two litters of four to eight piglets every twelve to fifteen months during a lifespan of four to eight years. A dozen piglets in the small herd had the potential to give birth to approximately eight-hundred and sixty-four total offspring over the course of their lives, a disturbing statistic.

Using their extra-long snouts, flattened and strengthened on the end by a thick plate of cartilage, they can root as deep as three feet and devour or destroy whole fields of sorghum, rice, soybeans, potatoes, melons and other fruits, nuts, grass, and hay. The hogs occasionally eat livestock especially lambs, goat kids, and newborn calves. They also, eat wildlife such as deer fawns and quail.

Because of their susceptibility to parasites and infections, wild hogs are potential carriers of disease. Swine brucellosis is the most problematic because of the ease with which it can be transmitted to domestic pigs and the threat it poses to the Texas pork industry.[6]

Walking along, periodically I stopped to look at my GPS and see where I was in relation to the brushy sendero where I had seen "El Viejo" a few days earlier. Soon, I reached a point directly below where I had seen him and the big doe. Carefully climbing out of the ravine, I started up the hill to the trail where I had seen them. As I quietly stepped around a large cedar bush, I saw a mangy looking coyote standing forty yards away slowly rocking his head from side to side, staring at me.

I stopped and watched as he began to walk very slowly towards me, wobbling unsteadily with each step. Annoyed, I thought, "Well hell! I don't want to shoot him with my rifle because the sound will likely alert any deer in the area of my presence."

The animal stumbled erratically in my direction, and I quickly realized that he was sick and exhibiting classic symptoms of rabies. Unlike the St. Bernard dog in Stephen King's 1983 movie "Cujo," the coyote was not wildly aggressive or biting everything around him; however, he was heavily panting, and his mouth was open and slobbering white foam. Usually, animals infected with the rabies virus will quickly die in freezing weather; however, not always and apparently that was the case here.

I slung the rifle over my shoulder and after removing my gloves reached under my coat for the Colt Diamondback .22 caliber pistol, I carried in a holster on my belt. Assuming the wide leg "Weaver stance," I carefully took both hands and lifted up the small revolver, placed the sights between the coyote's two eyes and slowly cocked the hammer. When the animal was approximately fifteen feet away, I steadily pulled the trigger and saw the CCI Stinger high-speed hollow point bullet strike where I had aimed. Instantly, he dropped to the ground and lay still.

I stood there for a while and then walked over to the coyote. Clearly, the animal had been sick for some time with large patches of blood-crusted mange covering most of his body and his exposed rib cage indicating he had not eaten in a long time. I was reluctant to let the carcass stay there because I knew later that night other varmints would come and eat the virus infected meat; however, I decided to leave it because I had no way of safely carrying it back to my truck and I certainly did not want to touch it. Holstering the revolver, I decided the sound of the pistol shot probably was quiet enough that it did not scare off "El Viejo," so I continued walking up the hill.

Near the top, I found numerous piles of deer droppings, with some being very fresh, but no other sign of the big deer. While walking along looking at the ground, I found a beautifully formed arrowhead and picked it up. It was a classically shaped point and probably was dropped by one of the Comanche's who roamed this area long ago with Quanah Parker's band. A few feet further along the rocky trail, near a large cedar tree, I began to smell the pungent, acrid scent of urine and next to the tree trunk was a pile of fresh cougar fecal droppings called "scat." Taking a stick, I spread it out and saw that it was still wet indicating it was dropped earlier that morning.

Frequently, the big cats will mark their territory by "spraying" urine on surrounding trees and bushes. Closely surveying the nearby terrain for any sign of it, I decided to be extra vigilant in my walk. After not seeing anything more in the sendero, I returned to my truck, picked up the remote-controlled "critter" equipment and drove back to the house.

Once inside, I took a small black cast iron "Dutch oven" pot of pinto beans, I had soaked the night before, poured the water out in the kitchen sink and replaced it with two containers of beef broth. After dicing a large Vidalia onion and cutting off the fatty tips of two pounds of bacon and placing them in with the beans, I turned the gas burner to low on the stove. Soon they began to gently bubble. I thought, "I'll let them slowly simmer all afternoon, and they'll be ready by dark when I come back." Before covering the pot, I added a can of diced tomatoes then seasoned the beans with salt, pepper and cumin powder. "I'll make another pan of cornbread for supper."

Going to the fireplace, I removed the screen and added several more logs. Then I went back to the kitchen and made a sandwich, opened a Dr. Pepper and sat down in the rocking chair by the fire. It occurred to me that in remembering my early boyhood hunting and shooting adventures, I was about to recall a point in time where my life would change dramatically. Sitting there for a moment, I felt a twinge of sadness thinking about the next event.

COYOTE HUNTER

ONE AFTERNOON IN EARLY JANUARY, after my sister and I got home from school, my mom sat us down in the dining room and told us that we were moving to Levelland, Texas in a couple of weeks. We were going to live with my grandparents until she could save enough money from teaching school to rent a house for us. She said that my father had moved to Randolph Air Force Base in San Antonio after Christmas and they were going to get a divorce. Penny began to cry, but frankly, I was relieved to know there were not going to be any further late-night arguments between my parents. A few weeks later, a small moving van arrived at the house early one morning and in a few hours loaded most of our furniture and personal belongings, which my mother, sister and I had packed.

A year earlier, I had received my driver's license because at that time Texas law allowed them to be issued to 14-year-olds. On the day of our move, I borrowed the car; packed my last four rolled up rattlesnake skins in a paper bag and drove to the western wear store where I had sold the others. I told the owner that I was moving and would not be selling him any more skins. He thanked me for holding up my end of the bargain, and I walked back to the car.

Pocketing the four twenty-dollar bills, I drove to the First National Bank down the street and after giving my savings book to the cashier withdrew all my rattlesnake earnings money, which amounted to almost twenty-three hundred dollars. The gray-haired elderly clerk, who I knew, tried to convince me not to close the account, but after telling her we were moving out of town, she put the money in an envelope and handed it to me.

I was saving the money in hopes of someday buying a used 1957 Chevrolet Bel Air two-door coupe, which was my dream car at the time. I stuck the envelope in the hip pocket of my blue jeans and returned home where I helped my mother finish packing the car.

Along with our suitcases and other personal items, I loaded the gun cases containing my 30-06 Springfield, my Model 12 Winchester shotgun, and my Savage over and under .22/410 in the trunk of the car. It was a dark overcast day, and the cold wind was blowing very hard from the north signaling a blue northern was about to arrive. From the direction we were going to be driving, a massive reddish-brown dust storm was approaching.

Closing and locking the front door and getting into the driver's seat of the car, my mother drove away from the house. I got a lump in my throat thinking about leaving my only friend Edward, who lived down the street, and moving again to another junior high school in the midterm. In eight years of schooling, I moved ten different times, so I was always the "new kid on the block" making it hard to find friends. Moving so many times as an "Air Force brat" was tough but it made me more self-reliant and independent than most kids my age.

Driving north out of town on Highway 87, we followed the moving van as it headed to Lamesa, Brownfield and then into Levelland, a distance of one-hundred-thirteen miles. Most of the farmland north of Big Spring was barren plowed fields, and as the wind increased, the dust storm reached us. The moving van slowed to fifteen miles per hour because the visibility had dropped to only a few feet. Soon the only thing we saw was the truck's two dimly lit taillights. I noticed my mother was tightly gripping the steering wheel with both hands and her knuckles were white. Sitting next to her on the front bench seat, I asked, "Mom, shouldn't we pull over to the side of the road and wait until the dust storm passes." Choking back tears, she replied, "No, I'm afraid if we stop on the side of the road somebody will run over us from behind." I realized then how emotionally difficult this whole situation was for her. But at the time, I didn't think there was anything I could do to help.

As we slowly followed the truck, I told her all the "knock knock" jokes that I knew and talked about everything I could think of until I ran out of things to say. Soon the car's heater began blowing a fine cloud of dust on both of us, so she asked me to turn it off and immediately the interior of the car began to get very cold. Penny was lying on the back seat with her head covered; wrapped in a quilt, my grandmother had given her.

After a while, I saw tears running down my mother's cheeks creating small rivulets in the fine dust on her face. Without saying anything, I took several tissues out of a Kleenex box on the dashboard, opened the thermos bottle she had filled with water and dampened them. Leaning over, I gently washed her face while she tightly held onto the steering wheel. I have never forgotten how sad and forlorn she looked as she thanked me and more tears began to flow. I decided then to do something to help ease her anxiety over having very little money. Reaching into my back pocket, I pulled out the envelope and said, "Here are all my rattlesnake skin earnings amounting to twenty-three-hundred dollars. I want you to have it to help us get settled in a new home. But, please don't tell anyone about this." She quietly began to sob, and big tears flowed from her eyes. After a few moments, she softly said, "Stan, Jr., you're a good boy, and you're going to grow up to be a fine man. Someday I may be able to give this back to you."

However, raising a family on the meager salary of a West Texas elementary school teacher in the early 1960s, she never saved anything and could not pay me back. It did not matter, and I loved her anyway.

Six hours later the dust storm began to clear, and we could see the road in front of us much better. Arriving in Levelland after dark, we pulled into the driveway of my grandparents' house, and they came running out to the car. We hugged them, and then everyone went into the warm house, which smelled of cornbread, pinto beans, and fresh-baked ham. After eating, I went out to the car and brought the suitcases and my guns inside. Later that night lying in the den on a rollaway bed, I choked back my tears thinking about giving up my dream of buying my first car but decided I had done the right thing and finally went to sleep.

The next morning my grandfather and I unloaded the rest of our belongings. Standing by the car, we were utterly amazed to see the windshield was frosted looking. The paint on the hood was gone, and only bare metal showed. The front chrome bumper was heavily pitted and dull looking too. Driving into the dust storm for six hours had completely sandblasted the front of the car.

Later that morning, my grandfather and I drove to a local dealership and left the car with them so they could replace the windshield and paint the front end. Walking back to his car, which I had driven, he turned to me and said, "Son, how would you like to become my chauffeur when you're not in school as I check out oil leases and new drilling locations here in west Texas and New Mexico?" "Sure, Granddad I would like that. Can I take my rifle and shotgun with us?" "Absolutely, you never know what we're going to find out there." He replied as he put his arm around me and squeezed my shoulder.

So, I began to drive my grandfather around to his various oil leases and locations on holidays and Saturday mornings. Frequently we went to Seagraves northwest of Lubbock, then back west to Denver City, Seminole, Hobbs, and Tatum, NM where he had oil wells and production facilities. One morning, as we approached a pump jack, I saw a coyote standing in a pasture fifty yards away from the white caliche road on which we were driving. "Granddad, can I shoot the coyote over there with my 30-06?" I asked. "Sure. Go ahead." He answered as he reached into the back seat and took the rifle out of its case. I chambered a round and rolled down my window. Setting the wooden forend of the gun on the door, I sighted through the peephole at the rear and placed the front post on the coyote's shoulder. Taking a deep breath, I let half of it out then squeezed the trigger. The gun went off with a loud "boom," and the animal instantly fell to the ground. We got out of the car and walked over to it. "Son, you know there is a bounty on coyotes, and the county agriculture extension agent will pay you ten dollars for each set of dead coyote's ears you bring him." He told me. "Really, Granddad," I exclaimed as I began to think about how I could replace my lost rattlesnake skin business with a new one involving coyote ears. "Yes and the ranchers around here will pay you five dollars for each carcass you hang on their fence line." Thinking back, I recalled seeing several coyotes as we drove through pastures over the past few weeks. I picked up the dead coyote by the stump of its tail, we walked back to the car, and I put it in an empty cardboard box in the trunk after cutting off both of its ears with my pocketknife.

Later that afternoon Granddad and I checked other oil well locations, then we drove to the ranch headquarters, and he introduced me to the rancher who owned the land. I told him about the coyote that I'd shot and he reached into his wallet and gave me a five dollar bill and asked me to hang the carcass on the fence by the asphalt road. I said, "Yes, sir I will." Then I asked, "Do you have many coyotes around here?" He answered, "We sure do, and I'll pay you five dollars for each one you kill." With that conversation, I started my new enterprise and began to build my savings again.

Each time I drove my grandfather I carried my rifle and several times shot two or three coyotes in a day. This meant that I was making thirty to forty-five dollars each time I drove for him. During the week, my grandfather went to the county seat, took the coyote ears to the agriculture agent, collected the bounty and gave it to me. It was not as much as I had earned with my rattlesnake skin business, but it gave me spending money for school and the local movie theater. One year later when I turned sixteen years old, I had saved five hundred dollars and bought a low-mileage blue 1957 Triumph TR-3 two-seater sports car. Today that car sells for between $30,000 and $40,000.

Chapter Eleven

ALMOST GOTCHA

DURING THE NIGHT, I AWOKE when it began to sleet heavily as another arctic cold front approached. The next morning at 5:00 am, I got up, dressed, then built a fire in the fireplace. Looking through the window over the kitchen sink, I saw a thick coating of ice built up on my pickup windshield, hood, and doors. Taking my keys, I remotely started the engine.

The wind was blowing approximately thirty miles per hour from the north again, and the temperature gauge by the door showed only two degrees Fahrenheit meaning the wind-chill was about minus twenty-three degrees. "Muchachos, it is going be colder than a well digger's butt today." I laughingly said aloud as I involuntarily shivered at the thought of spending the day walking through the deep sendero where I was now convinced "El Viejo" bedded down at night.

After breakfast, I washed the dishes and then put on my down vest over my Capilene-insulated undershirt. With my expedition weight parka on, I was now able to stay warm down to minus thirty degrees below zero. "Hopefully, the fur-trimmed hood will keep my head warm," I thought although I was wearing a navy colored wool watch cap.

Then I remembered a funny story I once read in a newspaper. In the mid-1960s the US Air Force Logistics Command decided to acquire seventy-five-thousand wolf pelts from American companies to make the parkas hooded fur rims. Soon after the announcement, the US Interior Department informed the Air Force that at that time there were not seventy-five-thousand living wolves on the entire North American continent.

The wolf species would have to be completely wiped out to fulfill the government requirement, thus creating an "ELE," which is an acronym meaning an "Extinction Level Event." PETA and the environmentalist had a "conniption fit" when they heard about it. The Air Force immediately canceled the request and instead began searching for companies that made synthetic fur. Today, all the military parkas that you see have that kind of hood.

Banking the coals, I placed the screen in front of the fireplace. Filling my thermos with hot coffee and stuffing several fried pies in my pockets, I walked out to the truck. It was heavily sleeting and snowing, and the frigid wind stung my face as I walked to the pickup. The ice built up on the pickup door made it difficult to open; however, after getting in and turning the heater up to high and the defroster on full blast, soon the windshield began to clear, and I drove away from the house.

I followed my dash mounted GPS to the senderos and parked where I had seen "El Viejo" and the big cat. Turning the engine off, I waited until it was light outside before I began my walk. I was determined finally to get a shot at the big deer. Soon the cab of the pickup was cold with snow and ice building up on the windshield. "Man, I'm going to have fun now." I grimly thought.

Although it was light enough to see, the visibility was only about fifty yards because of the blowing snow and sleet. I got out of the truck, checked to make sure there was a round in the chamber of my rifle and the safety was on, and then slung it over my right shoulder. Pulling the hood of my parka tightly over my head, I began walking down into the large ravine. The howling wind was blowing very hard directly into my face so I was sure the sound of my steps could not be heard nor would my scent be detected by "El Viejo." After walking for a few minutes my eyes began to tear up badly from the cold wind, so I returned to the truck and retrieved a pair of clear ski goggles that I frequently used when my wife and I went to Steamboat Springs, Colorado skiing. "Ah, that's much better," I thought as I wrapped a long dark green turtle fur scarf around my throat and again entered the sendero.

After two hours of slowly walking, I reached a small clearing next to the dry creek bed and sat down on a tree stump to rest. "Snotcicles" had formed on my mustache under my nose and my eyebrows and beard were coated in ice. I smiled as I thought, "I probably look like the Eskimo Nanook from the north with all the snow on my face." Fortunately, the gear that I was wearing kept me comfortable. In each pocket, I had a small stainless steel catalytic heater to warm my hands. The fuel that powers them lasts about seven hours before needing to be replenished. Additionally, I was wearing a pair of rechargeable lithium battery powered heated socks to keep my feet warm.

After resting for a few minutes, I slowly stood up and started to take a step then immediately froze (no pun intended) in place when I saw a large deer bedded down under a cedar bush about forty yards away. Standing there, I saw that it had a very large rack of horns with multiple points and two drop tines on each side of the main beams. "It's "El Viejo" bedded down." I thought. The deer was facing away from me with its head into the wind. "This is perfect. The harsh wind is covering my sound and my scent, so he doesn't know I'm here."

The deer was enormous with a dark mouse gray colored hide and snow covering its back and horns. "That's strange; he looks like a Currier and Ives Christmas card I once saw of a snow-covered deer bedded down in a Vermont forest." I thought.

Very slowly I unslung my rifle and moved it to my shoulder and looked through the amber protective lens caps installed on the objective and rear lens. "Oh no!" I softly exclaimed when I realized that ice was covering both of them and I couldn't see through the clear plastic eyepieces. Carefully, I released the front spring-loaded lens, and it popped open. I tried to do the same with the rear one; however, it would not come loose because it was frozen in place with ice. Slowly lowering the gun, I desperately tried to open the rear lens protector. Finally, it popped open, and as I looked up, I realized "El Viejo" was standing there staring straight at me.

We made eye contact, then he snorted loudly, blowing steam out of his nostrils and stomping his front hooves while shaking his enormous, snow-covered horns. "Oh my gosh, you are a magnificent animal." I thought.

"Snicking" the safety off with my right thumb, I slowly raised the rifle to my shoulder, but as I moved, the big deer instantly wheeled away on its hind legs and disappeared behind the large cedar bush under which he had been bedded down.

Standing there, awestruck at having found "El Viejo" again, I finally turned the safety back on my rifle, closed both of the lens caps and decided to walk back to my truck. Reaching into my pocket, I realized I had left my GPS in the truck. "Oh. Great, now I have to navigate back without really knowing where I'm going."

With the low visibility from the blowing snow, I really could not see very far in front of me; however, I began walking in the direction from which I had come.

Two hours later, I climbed out of the sendero, but my pickup was nowhere to be found. The visibility had dropped to "zero, zero" (as they say in aviation terms) because of the blinding blizzard, which was raging around me. Then I remembered, "If I remotely start my truck I will probably hear the Magnaflow* glass pack mufflers. After taking my heavy gloves off, I reached into my parka pocket, retrieved the keys, pressed, and held down the remote start button. Instantly, I heard the big 488 cubic inch, V-10 motor briefly turn over, then the deep throaty growl of the two mufflers as the engine started.

The sound was coming from the left of me, and I began walking in that direction. Within a few minutes, I arrived at the idling truck. Relieved, I unslung my rifle, opened the ice-encrusted door and got in the driver's seat of the vehicle, placing the gun barrel down in the passenger seat floorboard. I sat there with the heater blowing on high speed and soon warm air filled the interior. Lowering the driver side sun visor, I saw in the attached mirror, that my eyebrows, mustache, and beard were coated in icicles and snow. Starting to chuckle, I remembered skiing one Christmas with my wife Peggy in Steamboat Springs, Colorado when we got separated after I lost a ski on a blue run. One hour later, after finding the ski with the help of some college kids, I finally arrived at the lodge and walked into the restaurant where she and a group of our friends were waiting for me.

Strolling up to the table, at first they did not recognize me because of all the "snotsicles" and snow in my beard from falling headfirst into the snow bank when I caught an edge. Everyone thought that I looked like I had just walked in from the North Pole as I sat down and tried to get warm.

Sitting in the idling truck, I began wiping my face with a yellow microfiber towel and removed all the ice and snow. There was a four-inch snow accumulation on the ground, so I decided to drive to the house and stay there the rest of the day until the blizzard passed.

Inside the cabin, I built a big fire, undressed and put on my "soft clothes" as my grandson Noble says. It had been an exhausting and frustrating day, but I was more convinced than ever that I would soon kill "El Viejo" after seeing him up close.

Then as I was fixing supper, I began wistfully to think, "Is that what I want to do?" "Here we have an incredibly beautiful animal that has lived a solitary life for many years in a remote ravine on an out-of-the-way ranch in West Texas passing his genes on to future generations of big deer. If he were living in a controlled high fence environment, the range management overseer would never let him be shot because of his spectacular breeding capabilities." Shaking my head, I figuratively brushed away the thought. "Stan, you're turning into a sentimental old fool as you get older. "El Viejo" is just another big deer and will soon be past his prime. You can memorialize his life by killing him and then having a full-bodied mount prepared by any number of world-class taxidermists in Texas. You've even got a perfect place for the trophy deer display in your home office in North Dallas."

But, suddenly I saw the irony of taking his life to "memorialize" it, and in my heart, I began to have doubts about shooting "El Viejo."

6666 GOOSE HUNTING

AFTER CHURCH ONE SUNDAY AFTERNOON, while I was in the garage changing the oil in my sports car, I heard the kitchen telephone ring and my uncle Jesse was on the line. It was mid-January, and a lot had happened the previous year.

The summer before, in July, my mother was watching the noonday soap opera "As the World Turns" on television with her mother, when suddenly "Grandmother" said that she had a severe headache and was going to lie down before lunch. A few minutes later, my mother went in to check on her and "Grandmother" was dead from a massive cerebral hemorrhage. At the time, I was sixteen years old and working at the McEntire "U" ranch near Sterling City, Texas for the summer.

My Aunt Sally was married to Mac McEntire, the ranch owner. After a neighbor lady reluctantly relinquished the telephone "party line" that linked several ranches together, my mother called my aunt and told her that their mother had passed away at noon. Mac and I, along with six Mexican cowboys, were "drenching" sheep in pens that had a long cement trough attached to them. The "sheep dip" operation took place behind the "horse lot" next to the large barn behind the house.

Sally came running into the lot hysterically screaming, "Mother is dead. Mother is dead." Consoling her as best he could, Mac and the three of us went back to the ranch house and packed for the one-hundred-forty-mile trip to Levelland.

My aunt and uncle had three children; my cousins, Pam, Mackey, and Melanie. After packing everyone's bags and loading everything in their station wagon. We headed to Levelland, with me following behind in my sports car.

Arriving later that night, I saw my dad's 1960 Ford Thunderbird parked in the driveway and learned that he and my mother were trying to reconcile their marital problems and get back together again. After the funeral took place a few days later in Caddo, Oklahoma we returned home. My mom and dad announced to my sister and me that they were going to re-marry the next afternoon at the local Justice of the Peace office and then we were all moving to Connally Air Force Base in Waco, Texas.

"What about Granddad?" I asked my parents. "He and Grandmother were married for over 40 years, and I don't think he should be left alone." My dad asked, "Would you like to move in with him and stay here for your junior and senior year of high school?" Pondering that for a moment, I said, "Yes. I'm tired of moving all the time, and I'll stay with him until I graduate." So, that is how I ended up living with my grandfather.

"Hello, Jesse. How are you doing?" I said after answering the telephone. "I'm doing great, Stan Jr. A friend of mine in the oil business in Midland, Bill Meeker has a fiancée Anne Windfohr whose great-great-grandfather started the Four Sixes Ranch, and they have invited me to hunt geese this next weekend. I am calling to see if you would like to meet me there and hunt with us. Can you drive over to the Four Sixes Ranch in Guthrie on Friday night?" He asked. "Sure that will be fun, but I need to ask permission to get off work from my boss at the Dairy Queen. Can I call you later this evening after I find out?"

"That will be fine. Let me know if you can get come. I'll talk to you later." Then we hung up.

I was working at the local DQ after school each day but was sure they would let me off to spend time with my uncle since I was working so many hours during the week. The owner of the fast food restaurant had attended church with my grandparents, and his wife had been a good friend and bridge partner of my grandmother. They also knew that I had moved in with my granddad and he and I were "batching it" until I graduated from high school.

After changing the oil in my car, I drove to the Dairy Queen and asked my boss "Clara" if I could get off that weekend to go hunting. She said that would be fine and to come to work after school on Monday. Later that evening I called Jesse's home in Midland and told him that I was going to come to the Four Sixes Ranch and hunt with him. "We're going to be staying at the main house, and you're going to enjoy seeing this place." He said. "Why is that?" I asked. "It was built at the turn-of-the-century and is huge with massive rooms, tall ceilings and wide verandas surrounding the exterior." Continuing on Jesse said, "You will also get to meet one my friends, Henry D. Lindsley III. He and I went to school together at the University of Texas and were members of the same fraternity Kappa Sigma. Six years ago, he married Chandler Roosevelt, the granddaughter of former President Franklin D. Roosevelt. They are great people and love to hunt birds. I told them about you winning the Calcutta at the Midland country club pigeon shoot, and they want to meet you." I said, "This sounds like fun. I'll drive to the ranch headquarters in Guthrie after school on Friday. How are you getting there?" I asked. "We are flying into their private airstrip near the ranch headquarters Friday afternoon," Jesse said.

The Four Sixes Ranch (6666) was started by Samuel "Burke" Burnett in 1900 with the purchase of three-hundred-thousand acres of land and then expanded with the addition of one-hundred-forty thousand more acres for a total of four-hundred-forty-thousand. (685 square miles) In 1917, he built "the finest ranch house in West Texas" at Guthrie. It cost $100,000, which was a considerable sum of money for the time and was built with stone quarried on the ranch. Most of the lumber was brought in by rail car to Paducah and then hauled twenty-seven miles by wagon to Guthrie.

With eleven bedrooms and twenty-thousand square feet, it was a great place to entertain guests. Such well-known visitors as President Theodore Roosevelt, Will Rogers, Wylie Post and others had stayed there. Later the John Wayne movie "McClintock" was filmed on the ranch and the famous movie star stayed at the house along with his costar Maureen O'Hara.

The home was filled with unusual items. In the main salon, were numerous hunting trophies, expensive art and personal items given to Burnett by his friend Quanah Parker and the Comanche chief's wives. Although Burnett had a large bedroom in the home's southeast corner, he generally slept on a cot in the back room of the sparsely furnished Four Sixes supply house, where he maintained an office.

In 1921, oil was discovered on Burnett's land near Dixon Creek, and his wealth increased exponentially. This discovery, and a later one in 1969 on the Guthrie property, significantly benefited the family ranching business. There is an old Texas saying that "Cows sure do thrive in the shade of an oil well." How true! How true!

At noon on Friday, after getting permission from my teachers to "skip" my afternoon classes, I went home, changed into clean blue jeans, and put on a new denim western shirt I had received at Christmas. I then packed my hunting clothes and my Model 12 pump action shotgun.

Granddad had not been home for four days and was in New Mexico overseeing his drilling crews as they spudded in an oil well near Tatum, New Mexico. With no way of contacting him, I wrote a note explaining that I was going to the Four Sixes Ranch in Guthrie, Texas to hunt geesegeese with Jesse. I placed a salt shaker on top of the note and left it in the middle of the kitchen table then made sure all the house doors were solidly closed shut, but not locked, before getting into my car.

I drove east from Levelland to Lubbock then to Ralls, Crosbyton, Dickens and finally over the Four Sixes Ranch cattle guard on the road leading up to the house outside of Guthrie. It was about one-hundred-twenty-four miles total distance. I pulled up to the main ranch headquarters in the late afternoon. The house was gigantic, and smoke was billowing out of all six chimneys. Climbing out of my low-slung sports car, I stretched, put on my cowboy hat then walked up to the front door where I heard people laughing and talking inside. Pressing the antique, ornate brass doorbell, soon the door was opened by a white-jacketed butler who asked if he could help me.

Taking off my cowboy hat with the narrow rattlesnake band around the crown and holding it in both hands, I quietly said, "I've been invited to hunt birds here with my uncle, Jesse Heath. May I see him, please?" "Yes, Suh. Please follow me and I'll take you to him." The kindly white-haired old black man said.

We walked into the large foyer of the house and then into the huge living room where a half-dozen people were drinking cocktails, smoking cigarettes and laughing together. The hardwood floors were very dark oak and had been polished to a high gloss. Most of the twenty-five-foot walls were paneled in dark reddish brown mahogany with very ornately hand-carved crown moldings at the top. Several walls had thickly padded burgundy colored silk fabric that was heavily brocaded. The room was stunningly beautiful and unlike anything I had ever seen.

Western art hung everywhere. There were many Charles Russell paintings of Native American Indian villages and several others showing cowboys on horseback roping wild-eyed steers. Two Thomas Moran paintings featured intense shades of bright sunlight shining on dramatic mountains and rock formations with dark foreboding clouds in the background. Frederick Remington paintings were prominently displayed depicting cavalry horsemen and dusty cowboys branding and working cattle. Several large bronze sculptures of his were scattered around the room sitting on massively styled walnut tables with elegantly crafted ball and claw feet.

Jesse saw me and came over holding a short, thick lowball glass filled with scotch and several small cubes of ice in it. We shook hands, and then he said, "I'm glad you could make it here for the goose hunting, and I think you're going to like my friends.

How about a coke, Stan Jr.?" He asked. We walked over to a corner bar where a white-jacketed bartender was standing behind it, and Jesse asked him to pour me a soda.

After the bartender handed me a tall highball glass with coke and ice in it, Jesse took me over to his friends and introduced me to everyone. They were sitting on long leather sofas placed around a huge coffee table in front of the most massive fireplace I had ever seen. It was big enough to stand up in if the fire was out.

Sitting there was William (Bill) Meeker who was engaged to Anne Windfohr (Little Anne) the great-great-granddaughter of the Four Sixes Ranch founder, Samuel Burke Burnett. On another sofa sat Henry D. Lindsley III who was married to Chandler Roosevelt Lindsley, the granddaughter of former President Franklin

D. Roosevelt. The Four Sixes Ranch manager, George Humphreys was also sitting there with a drink in his hand. He was a 62-year-old, wiry-looking white-haired cowboy who had worked at the ranch since he was eighteen years old; a total of 44 years. George had arranged our hunting excursions for the next day.

Bill Meeker said to me, "Jesse told us about you winning the live pigeon shoot at the Midland country club two years ago when you were fourteen years old. How did you manage to do that?" Taking a sip of my Coke, I smiled and said, "It was easy. I just hit all the pigeons the Mexican threw."

Everyone laughed at that and Bill said, "Well, I sure don't want to be anywhere near you when we're hunting tomorrow because you will shoot better than I will." I decided that I liked Jesse's friends and especially the easy-going Bill Meeker.

Quietly sipping my Coke, I was enthralled by the stories everyone told about hunting big game in Africa and birds in South America. Clearly, I was in the presence of world-class adventurers who had traveled the globe on hunting expeditions. Coming from my humble background, I doubted that I would ever be able to afford those kinds of expensive trips. However, two days later when I returned home, I vicariously traveled the world as I became an avid reader of hunting books I checked out from my high school library and the one in downtown Levelland. I especially enjoyed reading Ernest Hemingway's, *Green Hills of Africa*, Jack O'Connor's stories of stalking North American game in *Outdoor Life* and *Field & Stream* magazines and Robert Ruark's two classic hunting books, *The Old Man and the Boy* and *Horn of the Hunter* both published in 1953.

Early that evening, the white-haired butler entered the room and announced that dinner was now being served. We all went into the dining room where there was a long table with fourteen chairs placed around it. On several sideboards, there were multiple hot chafing dishes with large cuts of rare-cooked prime rib floating in steaming au jus, slow roasted chicken covered in barbecue sauce, thick venison tenderloin "back strap" steaks and a wide variety of salads, fresh vegetables, and desserts. The array of food was staggering. After eating mostly hamburgers and drinking shakes or milk at the Dairy Queen where I worked after school, I was very hungry for something different.

Sitting down at the dining room table next to "Little Anne," who was only six years older than me; I waited until everyone was seated before I rapidly began to "wolf" down my food. She looked over at me and laughingly said, "Stan Jr. you are eating as if your stomach thinks your throats been cut."

Turning beet red in embarrassment, I slowly set my fork down and mumbled an apology. She put her hand on my forearm and earnestly said, "No, No, I'm teasing you! It's okay; we have lots of food so eat as much as you want." Turning to the butler standing behind her, she said, "Make sure he goes home with plenty of leftovers from tomorrow night's supper, so he won't have to eat hamburgers for a while." At that moment I believe I fell in love with the beautiful and vivacious "Little Anne" Windfohr although I never saw her again and in May, she married William "Bill" Meeker, my Uncle Jesse's close friend.

After dinner, we all "retired" to the living room and the bartender poured everyone, including me, XO (extra old) Louis XIII Remy Martin cognac in short traditional snifter glasses that ballooned at the stem. I took a sip and was pleasantly surprised at how smooth the amber-colored liquor tasted; later I learned that it was one-hundred years old and cost $2,400 per bottle.

Finishing the contents of the glass, I told Jesse that I was going to bring my clothes and gun into the house and take them to the bedroom where we were sleeping. Jesse said, "Everything's already been brought in and placed in our bedroom which has two large beds in it." "Oh, okay, then I'm going to go to bed now," I told him. Standing up, I thanked "Little Anne" for the evening and said goodnight to the other guests. The butler led me upstairs to one of the bedrooms where Jesse and I were going to sleep. During the night, two other couples arrived from Fort Worth and Dallas. However, their names have been lost somewhere in the fog of time as I have grown old.

At 5:00 AM the next morning, I was awakened by knocking on the door announcing that coffee and breakfast was being served in the dining room. Putting on my long handled underwear, I slipped into my flannel-lined jeans and then taking a tan colored chamois shirt from my suitcase, I put it on and tucked the shirttail into my pants. Telling Jesse I would meet him downstairs, I took my Winchester Model 12 shotgun out of its case, grabbed my hunting coat, shotgun shells and left. I set everything by the front door then walked into the dining room.

"Little Anne" and Bill Meeker were sitting at the table with Henry and Chandler Lindsley. "Good morning, everyone," I said as I poured a cup of black coffee for myself. Sitting down next to Bill, he leaned over and asked, "Are you ready to slay the wily goose?" "Yes, sir, I am if they will fly within seventy-five yards of me," I answered confidently.

"What kind of shotgun shells are you using that can reach out that far?" He asked. "Two and ¾ inch, High Brass, Winchester Super X number 2 size shot with 1¼ ounces of lead pellets," I said. Slowly shaking his head, he said, "Stan Jr., I want to see you do that." Later that morning he did.

Jesse walked into the dining room, poured himself a cup of coffee and sat down at the table. He and Bill began talking about two new oil wells they were drilling in the "Sprayberry play" south of Midland. The well locations were in the Permian Basin, a three-hundred-mile expanse of rich oil reserves stretching from southeastern New Mexico, and including Midland, Odessa and Fort Stockton in Texas, and Carlsbad, New Mexico.

George Humphreys, the ranch manager, came in and poured himself a cup of coffee, then sat down at the table. He told everyone that three, four-wheel-drive International Harvester Travelall's, each seating six people, were parked out front and the drivers would take us to some maize fields that had been harvested that fall.

"There are several cement lined pits with camouflage netting tops placed around the field where you will hunt. Let's head'em up and move out, everyone." He said. Then he left the room. I put several warm biscuits in a paper napkin, stuck them in my jacket pocket and walked out the front door after picking up my shotgun and gear. Jesse walked out carrying a hard-sided leather gun case containing a beautifully engraved pre-World War II Merkel 304e over and under shotgun with four sets of barrels. They were 12 gauge, 16 gauge, 20 gauge and 410. He purchased the firearm for $25,000 the year before at a gun store in Midland.

Bill Meeker, "Little Anne," Jesse and I climbed in one of the Travelall's and were driven a few miles to a maize field. It was still dark, so the driver parked the truck with lights shining on the pit, which allowed us to see as we went down the steps to the cement bottom where there were several folding chairs set up. Telling us he would be back in a few minutes, he drove away and parked the Travelall beneath some large mesquite trees about a quarter of a mile away.

Sitting in the dark, because no one had thought to bring a flashlight, we felt the bitterly cold wind blowing through the camouflage mesh-netting top. At the house, George told us the temperature was eighteen degree, and the wind was blowing twenty-five miles per hour, so the wind-chill was minus four degrees.

"Hace muy frio en aqui." (Spanish: "It is very cold in here.") I said to no one in particular. Jesse explained to Bill and "Little Anne" that I learned to speak fluent Spanish while working on a ranch each summer for my uncle, Mac and Aunt Sally. Bill said to me, "Ah. That explains why you look like a cowboy."

I grinned and said, "I guess so; however, I want to study geology and petroleum engineering in college and get into the oil business like Jesse and several other men in my family." After sitting in the dark for a few seconds, Jesse said, "It is a tough business, Stan Jr. and I doubt that the price of oil will ever exceed five or ten dollars a barrel." Of course, he was wrong, and years later, the price was one-hundred thirty-eight dollars per barrel.

Our driver and guide opened the camouflage top and stepped down into the blind carrying several flashlights, but no gun of his own. He had several goose calls on lanyards hanging around his neck. Quietly he said, "The geese will begin to move into the fields soon. There are fifty full-bodied decoys sitting twenty yards in front of this blind. When they set their wings to land, I will open the nettop, and everyone can shoot. You are only allowed to kill two lesser Canadian geese per day, so it will not take us long to fill our limit. Go ahead and load your shotguns now." Then he handed out the lights.

I placed a shotgun shell in the chamber of my gun and then inserted one in the magazine as well. Making sure the safety was on, I sat in the cold chair eagerly awaiting the time when we could begin to shoot. Soon we started to hear thousands of geese "honking" as they approached the grain fields. The guide slightly pushed open the nettop and started to blow his goose call loudly. As the birds drew near the sound was incredibly loud.

Then we began to hear their wings flap as they started to land among the decoys. Quickly looking at his watch the guide announced, "It is official. You can shoot now." Peeking through the netting, he said, "Here they come, get ready, get ready. Now shoot!" Then he threw open the camouflage netting, and all four of us stood up and began to shoot. The two geese I aimed at were close together, but around sixty yards away, so I fired two quick shots and knocked them both down. They hit the ground with a "thud," "thud" and lay still. Bill and Jesse each hit one bird and "Little Anne" shot one that landed in the decoys. The guide said, "Here come some more so reload." I started to put two shells in my shotgun when he said to me, "Hold up kid you've already shot your limit." Disgruntled, I sat down and thought, "Well, this has not been very much fun." The guide quickly opened the nettop and said, "Get them." The others each shot, killing three more geese. "That's all folks. We are done!" he said as he crawled, out of the pit and started gathering up the dead birds.

After climbing out of the blind, I walked over and picked up my two birds lying on the ground. They were heavy and fat from eating the maize that had fallen on the topsoil during harvesting. The guide went to the Travelall and brought it to where we were standing. After placing all the birds in cardboard boxes in the back, we all got in the vehicle and drove to the ranch headquarters.

For lunch, I ate a thickly sliced roast beef sandwich with potato salad and coleslaw while visiting and talking to everyone. In the afternoon, I played billiards with several of the men there but was beaten at every game. Obviously, they had spent a lot more time in pool halls than I had.

That evening we went into the dining room and were served the largest ribeye steaks I had ever seen. Each was over two inches thick and covered the entire plate. They were bigger than most of the pot-roasts my mother cooked for Sunday supper for the three of us. The sideboard had heated chafing dishes with steaming hot mashed potatoes, baked potatoes, and roasted vegetables. Sitting beside them was an assortment of salads, desserts, and steak sauce condiments. After dinner, several couples began to play bridge, and I excused myself and went to bed.

The next morning I awoke early, quietly dressed, so I would not wake Jesse, and went downstairs to drink coffee. No one was up, so I filled my cup, walked into the living room, and sat down in a high-back leather chair next to the fireplace. It was very peaceful and quiet, and I sat there staring into the fire grateful that I had been invited to the ranch. However, I decided not to hunt with the others again that morning because frankly, it was too easy and boring.

Midmorning, after everyone returned from the fields, I carried my shotgun out to my car and loaded my suitcase and hunting gear. The butler came out carrying a large heavy cardboard box filled with dry ice and containers of frozen geese breasts, uncooked rib eye steaks, salad and several pecan pies. After saying goodbye to everyone, I left and headed back to Levelland, anxiously looking forward to telling Granddad all that I had seen and done at the Four Sixes Ranch.

I was glad to have met all of Jesse's friends, especially "Little Anne" and Bill Meeker. Tragically, six years later, on May 3, 1968, Braniff International Airways Flight 352 was en route from Hobby Airport in Houston to Love Field in Dallas, when the Lockheed L-188 Electra broke up in midair and crashed near Dawson, Texas. It was carrying five crewmembers and eighty passengers including Bill Meeker; there were no survivors. The accident was the result of the captain's decision to fly into a violent thunderstorm, which over-stressed the airframe. A wing separated after the airplane lost control during a steep 180-degree turn the pilot made in an attempt to avoid the deadly weather. "Little Anne" Windfohr Meeker became a widow at the age of twenty-eight.

Arriving at home in the afternoon, I walked into the kitchen and saw a note from Granddad telling me that he was in Colorado City and would be home in about a week with some exciting news. I unloaded the car and put the geese and steaks in the outside chest style freezer. A few days later he called me one evening and said that he had married a friend of my grandmother's, Eula Mae Fuller, and they were moving to Stephenville, Texas as soon as his house in Levelland sold. We talked for a few minutes then we hung up, and I sat there in stunned silence.

The next day I went to school and then to work. Bessie Kitchens, the short, heavy-set elderly cook at the DQ, lived alone in an old, small three-bedroom frame house outside of town. I arranged to rent a room from her for twenty-five dollars per month, and a few weeks later, I moved into her home and lived there until I graduated from high school sixteen months later. Driving back to Granddads house after work I remember glumly thinking, "The only things that stay the same in my life are the changes." "Pero, realmente no importa." (Spanish: "But, really it doesn't matter.")

Chapter Twelve

COLLEGE, US ARMY AND YONDER

IN JUNE OF 1963, AFTER I graduated from Levelland High School I drove to Waco, Texas to visit my mom, dad, and sister Penny. I had decided that I wanted to attend Texas Technological College in the fall because several of my high school classmates were going there. Sitting at the dinner table that evening, I told my parents that I was not going to go to the University of Texas as they wanted me to, but instead, I was going to Texas Tech. Slowly nodding his head, my dad said, "Son, I'll tell you what I'll do. If you go to "UT," I'll pay for it, but if you go to Tech, you'll pay for it!"

For a while, we sat there discussing my choice of schools, but I was adamant about going to Tech. The next morning I loaded my car, said goodbye to my family, and drove back to Lubbock where I rented a room in a boarding house located next to the campus. For the next four years, I worked two jobs daily to pay for all my college and living expenses. However, between going to class full-time, taking at least 15 hours per semester, and working eight to ten hours per day including weekends, I did not have any time for hunting.

Then in 1967 I was drafted into the US Army and applied for, and was accepted, into helicopter pilot training. After graduating from flight school, I was sent to South Vietnam in February 1968 as a combat helicopter pilot just in time for the infamous "Tet

Offensive." After my first eighteen-month tour, I was transferred to Germany for two years and then volunteered to return to Vietnam and fly for the CIA for another eighteen months.

In 1974, I resigned my commission as an infantry captain when I learned that I would not be flying for at least five years because I had seven-thousand-four-hundred hours of helicopter and airplane flight time, which was significantly more than most current US Army aviators.

After leaving the military and for the next forty years, I became a banker ultimately owning several banks, investment banking firms, residential mortgage companies and commercial finance operations. From 1975 to 1982, I leased 20,000 acres in West Texas where I took bankers, real estate developers, attorneys, and business associates hunting for deer, quail, and turkey. I bought a four-bedroom doublewide modular home for my guests and me to stay in and placed it on the lease at the end of a four thousand foot dirt airstrip I had built so that we could fly in and out in our private airplanes.

In 1995 while living in North Dallas, my wife Peggy bought me a membership in the renowned Dallas Gun Club where I began shooting in competitive sporting clay events. Five years later in June 2000, I loaded my new Yukon XL SUV with four shotguns and twenty-thousand rounds of target shells and competed in the state championship tournaments of Louisiana, Mississippi, Alabama, Florida, Georgia, North Carolina and Kentucky. Although I never was the "winner," I always finished in the top ten percent and as Granddad would say, "a good time was had by all!"

After college and the military, I never became a big game hunter like Jesse's friend George Landreth or the people I had met at the Four Sixes Ranch. However, I had several opportunities to hunt enormous flights of dove in Argentina and Mexico and enjoyed shooting pheasant in Kansas, mule deer in Colorado, elk in New

Mexico and plantation quail in Georgia. *In short, I've had a real good time hunting, all of my life!*

GOTCHA

LEANING AGAINST THE SLENDER POPLAR tree, I had "El Viejo" in the crosshairs of my scope. He was standing approximately eighty yards away in a flat area next to the snow-covered riverbed grazing on ryegrass. With my left hand, I adjusted the scope to twelve power, and his body nearly filled the objective lens. I had removed my right glove, so with my thumb, I gently push the safety off and placed my right index finger on the Sako's two-pound trigger. Adjusting my aiming point, I placed the four-plex crosshairs slightly behind his right shoulder midway between the top of his back and the bottom of his chest. Taking a deep breath, I let half of it out and then began to apply pressure on the trigger with the tip of my finger. "El Viejo" was completely unaware that he was about to die!

The arctic cold front had finally passed taking with it the sleet and snow and now and the morning was bright but very cold. My plan for finally confronting "El Viejo" had worked flawlessly. After breakfast, I made two sandwiches, put them and my last two fried pies in a paper sack, and filled my thermos with coffee. I walked out to my truck, which I had already started and sat down in the driver's seat.

Earlier that morning before leaving the house, I looked at the large topographical map of the ranch and saw that I could drive to the far end of the canyon and then walk back to the entrance at the opposite end where the ground stand and the critter decoy were located. I set a GPS waypoint for the new location.

I first drove to the food plot and climbed the ladder to the deer stand and opened the back door. I duct taped the locking mechanism so the door would not stay shut. After climbing down the ladder, I watched as the wind slammed the door shut, then opened it, then shut it again. The noise of the banging door could be heard for a long distance.

Getting back in my truck, I drove to the ground stand set up near the sendero where I had first seen "El Viejo" and the big cougar. Stepping out, I took my battery-operated "critter getter" and set it next to a cactus thirty yards in front of the camo stand and switched it on. Immediately the furry animal decoy began to flop erratically around on the ground making a soft rustling noise.

Finally, I drove to the new waypoint that was about two miles from where I had last seen the big deer in the snowstorm the day before. I turned the ignition off and waited for it to become light enough before I began my stalk. "Today is the day this old man is going to challenge the other old man," I muttered resolutely to myself.

At 6:30 a.m., I exited the truck; making sure there was a cartridge in the gun's chamber, the safety was on, and both of the yellow plastic lens covers were open. After slinging the rifle over my shoulder, I started walking into the sendero prepared to trek the entire six-mile distance back to my ground stand if I needed to. I carefully placed every footstep as quietly as possible. Several times, I saw the sudden flash of whitetail deer as they ran to avoided me.

The sandy river bottom was covered with light snow, which helped to muffle my steps. Every ten minutes I stopped and did not move at all until a few minutes had passed. Then I slowly began to walk again. At 8:00 a.m., the sky was a deep cobalt blue and the morning sun cast brilliant white rays on the snow-covered cedars, poplar trees and mesquite branches causing them to glisten and sparkle with diamond-like qualities.

Stopping once more, I waited and then saw movement just as I was beginning to take a step. Standing there, I waited and did not move at all. One minute passed; then two, then five and still I saw no further movement. Finally, "El Viejo" stepped into the dry creek bed and began to paw at the vegetation under the snow and graze. Captivated, I watched as he occasionally raised his head and blew the snow off his large bulbous black tip nose when he snorted.

Watching "El Viejo" through my riflescope with my index finger lightly touching the trigger, I felt a gentle cold breeze blowing on my face. The air was clean and fresh with the sweet smell of cedar evergreens and their pungent amber sap permeating the ravine. I thought of the ancient Native American mantra, "Today will be a good day to die." Unexpectedly I got a lump in my throat.

This end of the sendero was tranquil, serene and almost like a cathedral with all the overhanging tree branches and sunbeams filtering through them. Looking at the big mule deer, I saw white hair on his ears and face which was a normal trait for his breed. Then I noticed that he had considerable loose, flabby skin around his face, and especially below his jaw.

With growing awareness, I realized I was looking at a buck, which was at least eight-years-old, as Charlie had first told me. Knowing a mule deer's lifespan in the wild is about ten years, it occurred to me that he only had at most two years to live. "All the more reason to harvest the animal." I rationally thought. Still, I hesitated to pull the trigger and kill the magnificent and regal looking buck.

Over the past ten days, our lives had become intertwined in a manner that I never expected. I relished the stalking and hunting of

"El Viejo"; however, I also enjoyed the solitude of the cabin, sitting in the creaking rocking chair listening to the sounds of the crackling fireplace and recalling my boyhood hunting adventures with men whom I truly loved and who loved me.

Nonetheless, the continual recalling of childhood memories had subtly transformed this "Old Man" and rendered me incapable of pulling the trigger. Then while standing there, everything became very still, and "Something" told me to release the pressure on the trigger. I immediately did so and lowered the gun barrel. Hearing the windblown poplar leaves above me begin to rustle, I imagined my Granddad, Dad, Jesse, Mac and my father-in-law Roy B. looking down at me, smiling and nodding their heads in agreement with my decision not to kill "El Viejo."

Slowly backing away from the tree, I turned and quietly began walking to my truck. Then I stopped, bowed my head and softly whispered, "El Viejo. Vaya con Dios por el fin esta cerca!" (Spanish: "Old Man. Go with God for the end is near!")

I am not sure if I addressed the deer or myself.

THE END

NOTES

[1] *The Old Man and the Boy.* Copyright 1953, 1954, 1956, 1957 by Robert C. Ruark, Jr. and renewed in 1981 by Harold Mason, Paul Gitlin and Chemical Bank, Executors of the Estate of Robert C. Ruark, Jr.

[2] *Hill Country Landowners Guide.* By Jim Stanley, Texas A&M University Press. 1978. Page 23.

[3] *Makin Tracks; A Year in the Life of the White-tailed Deer* November 6, 2010. School of Forest Resources, University of Georgia. George Wilhite, Doctoral Thesis, Page 45-48.

[4] Texas Parks and Wildlife Department: Online Guide to Western Texas Wildlife.

[5] Arizona Game and Fish Department. Quail hunting and seasons.

[6] www.smithsonianmagazine.com/science-nature/a-plague-of-pigs-in-texas

www.ingramcontent.com/pod-product-compliance
Lightning Source LLC
Chambersburg PA
CBHW021828090426

42811CB00032B/2065/J